Department of Health and Social Security

SOCIAL WORK DECISIONS IN CHILD CARE

Recent Research Findings and their Implications

LONDON HER MAJESTY'S STATIONERY OFFICE

© *Crown copyright 1985*
First published 1985
Fifth impression 1987

ISBN 0 11 321046 9

Contents

Foreword

A substantial body of research commissioned by the Department of Health and Social Security and by the Economic and Social Research Council into aspects of work with children in care has recently been completed. The research represents the product of a considerable investment of time, skill and knowledge and the results merit close attention. Research is sometimes criticised for not reflecting the contemporary concerns of practitioners. To overcome this a group of practitioners and middle managers were asked to examine the material and to extract the "messages" that answered their needs. This work has led to the report which is the main body of this publication. Jane Rowe has been mainly responsible for writing the report, and her assistance throughout has been invaluable.

The aim of this publication is not to report research findings in detail. It aims to pull out of several research reports the common findings which have a bearing on professional and practice issues regarding social work decisions about children and care. It does not offer easy solutions but, if professional judgement is to operate at a uniformly high standard, many of the issues raised warrant careful consideration.

Some "Is it true for us?" exercises have been devised in order to help managers and practitioners test practice in their own agencies. It is hoped that these practical aids, which do not claim to be scientific or exhaustive, will help to answer the questions that the research raises.

Social work with families and children is complex, difficult and sometimes painful. Families whose children are either in the care of the local authority or on the verge of care face many great difficulties. High professional standards, mature experience and sophisticated social work skills are needed to help such families. Sensitive and knowledgeable work by professional social work practitioners is required to secure a practical partnership with parents which will operate in the best interests of the children. The search for continual improvement must go on if high standards of practice are to be achieved and maintained. The research offers valuable leads and raises many pertinent questions.

Although the research relates to social work practice in England, other parts of the United Kingdom may find the document of interest and relevance to their experience.

W. B. Utting

W. B. UTTING
Chief Inspector Social Services Inspectorate
Department of Health & Social Security

PART I   Introduction

The period 1983/84 saw the completion of a number of child care research studies which were funded by the Department of Health and Social Security and the Economic and Social Research Council. These studies covered a variety of subjects but the topic of social work decisions in child care was important in many of them and central to several. Both funding bodies put a high priority on dissemination of the research findings and plan a variety of activities to that end for example, a seminar programme, development projects, and the funding of training materials. The Department has also used the research as an information base in policy revision.

As a first step in dissemination, the Department decided to call together a working party of experienced social work practitioners who could offer a critical appraisal of the relevance and importance of the research findings and consider how these might best be brought to the attention of policy makers, managers, practitioners and social work educators. Members of the working party met on five occasions during the winter of 1984/85 and the main part of this paper is the result of their study and deliberations.

Nine studies were considered by this group, eight funded by the DHSS and one ('In and Out of Care') funded by the ESRC.

Of the nine selected studies, four are either primarily concerned with decision making or provide crucial insights. These are:

1 *WHO NEEDS CARE? — Social work decisions about children*
   Jean Packman, John Randall and Nicola Jacques
   Blackwell — Due Spring 1986

2 *CHILDREN LOST IN CARE — The family contacts of children in care*
   Spencer Millham, Roger Bullock, Ken Hosie and Martin Haak
   Gower — Due Autumn 1985

3 *IN CARE — A study of social work decision making*
   Jeni Vernon and David Fruin
   NCB — Due Autumn 1985

4 *IN AND OUT OF CARE — The experience of children, parents and social workers*
   Mike Fisher, Peter Marsh and David Phillips with Eric Sainsbury
   Batsford/BAAF — Due 1986

There are two further studies which have findings of direct relevance to decision making although this was not their central concern. These are:

5 *LONG TERM FOSTER CARE*
   Jane Rowe, Hilary Cain, Marion Hundleby and Anne Keane
   Batsford/BAAF — 1984

6 *DECISION MAKING IN STATUTORY REVIEWS ON CHILDREN IN CARE*
   Ruth Sinclair
   Gower — 1984

The three remaining studies provide useful supportive data and give balance and strength to the overall picture.

7   *SOCIAL WORKERS AND SOLICITORS IN CHILD CARE CASES*
Linden Hilgendorf
HMSO — 1981

8   *THE ADMINISTRATIVE PARENT* — *A study of the assumption of parental rights and duties*
Margaret Adcock, Richard White and Olwen Rowlands
BAAF — 1983

9   *THE IMPLEMENTATION OF SECTION 56 OF THE CHILDREN ACT 1975*
(Unpublished research report)
Olive Stevenson and John Smith

The deliberations of the working group were interpreted, and translated into a written report, by Jane Rowe whose skill and depth of understanding were greatly appreciated. The report was originally intended for an internal DHSS audience but its content inevitably indicated a need to make it available to a much wider audience.

In this publication, the text of the group's report is supplemented with two other contributions. Part II consists of single page summaries of their research findings prepared by the authors. Although these summaries are helpful, they do not do justice to the research. Most project reports provide a wealth of qualitative and sensitive detail about dealing with children who are considered for or admitted to care. They merit careful reading in full.

The final section of the report, True for Us?, suggests ways by which managers and practitioners in individual social services departments can find out whether some of the concerns raised by the research apply on their own patch. Although between them the research reports covered a wide spectrum of authorities, variations in practice and recent changes will undoubtedly mean that certain issues raised by the research apply more strongly in some places than in others.

It is well understood that social services departments are currently facing a range of important issues and a further complexity is that these research studies focus only on families with children, whereas social work practice in many areas is not structured with the same boundaries. However, child care is predominant in many work loads and a number of the issues raised here translate to other client groups. Whatever the local situation, some of the concerns raised in this paper and drawn from the significant research reports must be high on the priority list for attention.

Because the research projects in total covered so many aspects of child care, the theme of SOCIAL WORK DECISIONS IN CHILD CARE has been adopted in order to set manageable boundaries and provide a focus for dissemination activities. Many of the messages of the research are not included in this summarising exercise but have been disseminated in published books and by the research authors themselves talking at conferences and seminars.

Within the chosen theme of decision making, several overarching concerns are identified by the research findings and are documented in the main section of the following text. These include: over-emphasis on admission to care; the importance of preventive services; the need for greater clarity and more congruence on the part of those involved about the purposes of care and the values and assumptions underlying it; the apparent passivity of social workers; the key role of case supervision; the balance between compulsion and control; and the value of developing policies which are clear and effective yet sufficiently flexible to allow for professional discretion in individual circumstances.

It is recognised that some of the findings of the research merely confirm familiar concerns, but systematic and recent evidence on these topics is nevertheless valuable. Some important findings are new while others provide subtle new insights into old problems. The working group considered why child care practice might raise such particularly intractable issues and have suggested reasons concerned with the painful, complex and long-standing nature of many child care cases; the difficulty of harnessing bureaucratic structures to provide individual parenting; the limited opportunity for social workers to acquire the sophisticated skills or have access to the quality of support required for confident work in this area; and the lack of a research base which would help practitioners predict the consequences of significant decisions.

There are no easy answers although some findings do seem to indicate clear and achievable general solutions. Other issues raised are likely to be most amenable to local development and resolution. It is hoped, too, that the positive steps the Department is taking, and which are touched on at the very beginning of this introduction, will contribute to the process of change. It is encouraging to emphasise views in some of the research reports that brave and imaginative work was being carried out with some vulnerable children and that in the working group's view, some improvement in practice is feasible by making even better use of available resources.

The total scope of DHSS and ESRC funded programmes of research includes projects not considered here which address issues of costs in child care, residential care and young people leaving care. As these studies come to fruition it is intended that they should be appropriately assessed and digested so that practitioners and their agencies can derive greatest benefit from the work carried out.

Research on Child Care
Working Party of Child Care Practitioners

List of group members:

Mr Maurice Phillips (Chairman)	Deputy Chief Inspector Social Services Inspectorate — DHSS
Mr C Davies	Principal Officer Children's Services Somerset County Council (ADSS nominated)
Mr R Dunster	Team Manager Warwickshire Social Services Department (BASW nominated)
Mr J Hopkins	Lecturer School of Social Work Keele University (SCA nominated)
Mr G Thompson	Senior Social Worker Bradford Metropolitan DC
Mrs B Warner	Director of Social Work Norwood Child Care
Mr P Riches	Assistant Director (Development) NCB
Mr F Loughran	Co-ordinator for ESRC funded research of children in care Bristol University
Dr J Packman	Senior Lecturer Social Work Department Exeter University
Miss J Rowe	Research Project Director BAAF
Mr R Hughes	Children's Division — DHSS
Miss P Barrett	Children's Division — DHSS
Mr D Stapleton	Social Services Inspector Social Services Inspectorate — DHSS
Mrs J Griffin	Principal Research Officer Office of the Chief Scientist — DHSS

Research Overview

I The Evidence

The cumulative evidence of these nine reports is weighty and convincing. The research was conducted in 49 local authorities and included about 2,000 children. Virtually all the findings point in the same direction. As one member of the practitioners' group put it, reading these reports is like looking out of different windows and seeing the same view. It has to be said that the scene portrayed is generally quite disturbing and depressing. Nevertheless, there is encouragement in the researchers' emphasis on improvements to practice which could be achieved even without the further resources which are needed to provide a really adequate service.

The practitioners in the working party are agreed that these research findings ring true for the current, overall social work scene even though the studies cannot provide an accurate picture of all aspects of child care in every social services department. There are also variations in practice between areas within one department and individual social workers may achieve a high degree of skill and effectiveness even if others in their department do not reach this standard. Since these research projects were carried out, some departments have moved forward to develop more explicit child care strategies and are working hard to include parents in planning. They are trying to promote preventive services and to make sure that children do not 'drift' into care. On the other hand, economic recession and resource constraints are creating additional pressures that militate against good practice. Although the research is mainly based on practice as observed in 1979–82, there is no reason to think that the findings are generally out-dated or irrelevant.

It is probably inevitable that research reports tend to have more to say about deficiencies than about aspects of a service which are going well and this can produce a misleadingly gloomy picture. This paper, too, concentrates on problems because they require urgent attention. But it would be a dis-service to the researchers on whose work it is based if it did not also reflect their deep understanding of the inherent difficulty and complexity of the social work task and the severe problems besetting social work practitioners. Criticisms of current practice and suggestions for change have to be considered:

(a) in the light of the particular focus of these research studies;

(b) in the context of our national economic problems, rapidly changing family patterns, a mass of new child care legislation and the re-structuring of many social services departments.

It is important, too, to emphasise the distinction between social workers' decisions and social work decisions since the latter may be required by management either as general policy or in a particular case. The focus of these research studies was on field social workers and their practice. Thus, far more attention was paid to their imperfections than to deficiencies in management styles and systems, though by inference it is often clear that much might be laid at management's door. Nor did the work of other carers (residential workers or foster parents) or of other agencies (police, schools, courts) come under the same sort of scrutiny. And finally, these research projects could not attempt to evaluate the part which the children's families played in the problems under discussion.

Clearly, it would be inappropriate as well as unjust to consider today's social workers as responsible for the unsatisfactory levels of child care revealed in these research reports. Nevertheless, their key position in decision-making, planning and in the delivery of service to children and families, must make them a prime target for the dissemination of the research findings. Politicians, administrators, social work educators and managers will, of course, have to take responsibility for implementing many of the necessary changes. But without the wholehearted support of social workers and their determination to increase their professional skills, the research recommendations are likely to remain a dead letter. It does, therefore, seem appropriate that this overview should reflect the researchers' emphasis on the role and responsibilities of social work practitioners even at the risk of sounding overly critical.

It is a measure of the quality and richness of the research studies, as well as of the complexity of the issues they address, that their findings cannot usefully be reduced to very brief summaries. In addition to the factual findings, a web of themes and concerns runs through and between the reports. Readers will distil their own priorities, but for the purposes of discussion some pattern has to be imposed.

It may be useful to compare the data to an apple. The skin, or most visible part, is made up of facts disclosed by the research about how social work decisions — or lack of them — affect children in care and their parents. Next comes a thick layer of flesh composed of the researchers' understanding of what lies behind these decisions. Their emerging ideas can be grouped into themes which are common to more than one study. In the centre, hidden from view, understandable only by deduction and difficult to prove, are the reasons or causes which form the core of the problem. None of the individual researchers was in a position to explore this core in any detail because it is only by studying the accumulated findings that basic issues become clear. But the practitioners' working party has been able to consider at least some of these core issues and can offer some suggestions about the implications for policy and practice.

The rest of this paper will consider in turn: facts and findings, the themes, and the core of basic issues.

II Facts & Findings

The facts which form the skin of our apple can be grouped under the headings A) Admission, B) The care experience, C) Practice issues and policy problems.

A) Admission
1) Social workers consider themselves primarily responsible for most decisions about admissions to care but are often under strong pressure from outside agencies or from the children's families.

   "Rarely in our study cohort of 450 children did social workers report that the decision to admit a child to care was out of their hands."
   (Dartington)*

   "It was apparent that within social services departments a key role was allocated to main grade social workers: basically it was they who determined who entered the department's care system. They, nonetheless, rarely executed this task feeling that they had any alternative and often only after long and sustained pressure from other agencies or even from the child's family."
   (National Children's Bureau)

   "Discussions with superiors were apparently understood in terms of advice, guidance, assistance or rubber-stamping... for seniors and

* The quotations in this document are taken from the research reports submitted to the DHSS.

managers were rarely credited with having taken prime responsibility for a decision (about admission)." (Packman)

2) Most decisions are made rapidly and often in crisis. As a result admissions are not well planned.

"Over half the decisions were made within a week and more than a third were made within twenty-four hours." (Packman)

"The precipitating crisis...was usually expected and in three-quarters of cases social workers felt that the referral was certain to lead to a care admission...Yet...the actual moment of the precipitating crisis seems to have come as something of a surprise...There seems to be a serious conflict between the wish to keep out of the care system and the rather haphazard strategy employed when admission becomes necessary." (Dartington)

(In relation to admission) *"Too often this was conducted in a way calculated to reinforce rather than reduce the shock and damage of separation for the children and young people involved. Long-established lessons of good child care practice...were honoured more in the breach than in the observance."* For example, pre-placement visits were achieved for only one in five voluntary admissions and almost none where admission was compulsory. In only half the voluntary admissions and 15% of compulsory cases did a parent accompany the child into placement. (Data from Packman)

3) There can be wide variability between authorities in patterns of referral, response and admission, but differences between children taken into care or kept out of care may be minimal. Delinquents are more likely to be admitted than are children 'at risk'.

"Pressures on the two departments were of a different scale and quality...Child care resources in the two authorities were strikingly different...A picture (builds up)...of two authorities...(with) different and distinct biases in their child care work. One leaned toward the teenage troublemaker...the other appeared to place more emphasis on the child at risk."

Nevertheless, in both authorities: *"There was little to distinguish the admitted group from the rest in terms of most child and family characteristics except parental ill-health; a child's difficult behaviour (in particular delinquency, truancy and running away); and a child's previous admission to care, which were all positively correlated with admissions. Concern over standards of parenting, risk to a child's health and development, presence on the 'at risk' register and a history of neglect and abuse were, however, significantly associated with avoidance of admission."* (Packman)

4) Compulsory powers (in particular Place of Safety Orders) are being used increasingly but often are counter-productive.

In 1962, less than half of the children in care had been admitted compulsorily or else their parents' rights had been taken over by the local authority. By 1980, the proportion had risen to three-quarters. Place of Safety Orders are now being widely used for children of all ages with 30% of children in the Packman study and 22% of the Dartington cohort entering care in this way.

In the two authorities studied by Packman, policies had clearly moved toward the use of compulsory admission for cases expected to be long-term. The National Children's Bureau study also highlights the departments' reliance on compulsory powers particularly when admitting older children.

"Although over half the admissions of older children were to voluntary care, the notion that the voluntary admission of adolescents was inappropriate was very powerful...(Social workers) waited for the opportunity of compulsory admission." (National Children's Bureau)

However, although the need for greater control is usually justified on the basis of better planning and stability, these studies show that it does not necessarily achieve this.

"Compulsion did not appear to lead to more achievable plans or to greater security for the children — at least in the short term. What it did achieve...was immediate 'control' over children, parents or both who were regarded as dangerous and disruptive." (Packman)

"Children entering care via this route generally have greater problems in maintaining links with their families and tend to stay long in care." (Dartington)

Compulsion could also have a damaging effect on relationships between parents and the department.

Parents whose children had been compulsorily removed felt that, *"They had little or no influence on the decisions that had been made,"* and at the 6 month follow up they *"continued to feel that matters had been taken out of their hands...Many also felt impotent to influence social workers' plans for their child."* (Packman)

Packman and the Dartington team found parents distressed, disgruntled even outraged by compulsion, though the Sheffield team, whose sample was more heavily weighted with adolescents, found parents less concerned about the legislative route to care than about whether their own problems, attitudes and feelings of responsibility had been properly understood. They say:

"It seems to us that there has been an over-emphasis on the issue of (parents') rights...and a neglect of the question of the appropriateness of care as a solution to the difficulties of families. Certainly the parents we interviewed were intensely interested in the latter question and saw the former as a non-issue." (Marsh & Fisher)

5) <u>The differing perspectives of parents and social workers may go unrecognised.</u>

"Often inadequate attention was paid to the history of the clients' problems, to issues of discipline and authority within the home, to parents' expectations of the workers' intervention and to establishing a knowledge base common to all participants. Too often, disagreements about the nature of problems and about methods of handling them remained unexplored undercurrents in exchanges between workers and clients...(This approach) was extremely unlikely to lead to substantial agreement over the <u>purpose</u> of care." (Marsh & Fisher)

"It seems probable that social workers quite often misinterpret natural parents' behaviour at the time of admission because the psycho-social study of the family is not sufficiently thorough...we have some painfully vivid examples of cases where parents were considered rejecting or uncaring because the problems they were facing had not been properly understood." (Rowe)

"In relation to parents, workers constantly underrated the amount of continued responsibility and concern they felt for their children, tending to misinterpret relief as rejection." (Marsh & Fisher)

6) <u>Parents requesting care for their children are 'put through hoops' in an effort to prevent admission and if admission is refused, few services are offered.</u>

(When parents requested care)...*"...alternative arrangements would be put forward by the social worker...the parents persisted...Care was viewed positively as a service by the families...but the social workers usually responded to such requests with hesitation and reluctance...(When) the parents themselves recognised that they wanted some form of help (to avoid abuse)...the child's admission was generally preceded by several requests for 'something' to be done. Admission occurred at the point where the parent abandoned the child or reported or threatened non-accidental injury."* (National Children's Bureau)

"The decision not to admit their children was seen (by the parents) in purely negative terms. Nothing helpful in their eyes had been offered in its place and some were left with a very real sense of despair...Thus Clayport's low admission rate fostered large numbers of disgruntled parents who felt unhelped and neglected." (Packman)

B) The Care Experience

1) <u>Far less attention is given to what is to happen after admission than to whether or not to admit and if children stay long in care, social work attention fades.</u>

"The system itself is geared towards placing an emphasis on the justification for intervention rather than what intervention would achieve." (Hilgendorf)

"This study has highlighted with considerable precision a situation that has long been known—that unless a child leaves care quickly, that is within six weeks—he or she has a very strong chance of being in care in two years time. Yet, the administrative arrangements within social services and social work practice often do not reflect this acutely short time scale. We find a time perspective entertained by social workers which is greatly at variance with the urgency experienced by the child and family or which, this study demonstrates, is in their best interests." (Dartington)

"Once a child has come into care and the earlier pressure from other agencies and individuals to admit no longer applies, there is a consequent relaxation in the priority accorded to the case by the social worker as attention shifts to more pressing cases.

...With a few notable exceptions, there is little evidence to suggest that planning becomes any more prominent an activity as time progresses." (National Children's Bureau)

(In the second six months of care) *"The earlier social work strategy of 'wait and see' now emphasises the 'wait' rather than the 'see', for social work activity shows a marked decline."* By 12 months only 36% of children were being seen fortnightly and only 17% of mothers were getting regular visits. (Dartington)

2) <u>Children in care are likely to experience many changes of placement.</u>

The instability of 'in care' placements is hammered home to the reader of these research studies by the depressing similarity of their findings.

"Four out of five admitted children had moved at least twice and a quarter at least four times, in the space of a few months." (Packman)

"In relation to their most recent admissions, 33% of children had two or three placement changes and 17% four or more." (Marsh & Fisher)

Over a two year period *"56% of the children will have had three or more placements and 14% of them will have had more than four."* (Dartington)

Some of these changes are due to the unplanned, emergency nature of many admissions, others to the use of a preliminary placement for assessment, but subsequent placements frequently break down or are found to be unsuitable. Thus Marsh points out that social workers who looked to residential care to provide consistent handling, secure limits and stability often found that structure became regimentation or that staff turnover and problems of hand-over between shifts mirrored the child's experience of inconsistent parenting at home. Problems over young people's disruptive behaviour in residential establishments often led to transfers.

The Dartington study reveals that of 170 children still in care after two years, 63 were thought by their social workers to be unsuitably placed. They report:—

"Transfer and breakdown of children in placements selected by social workers are common... This propensity to breakdown is only slightly less common among young children than adolescents and is as likely to occur in foster as in residential care... Seven out of the fifteen infants admitted to care before the age of two have suffered a placement breakdown, three of them under crisis conditions." (Dartington)

3) <u>Discharge or remaining in care is not usually the result of social work planning.</u>

"Remaining in care is not always the outcome of a decision, but may be the outcome of not taking a decision... It was rarely possible to pin-point when, or how, the decision that they would not return home had been taken... Many children remained in care or in a particular placement, not as the result of an explicit decision that this would be the best course of action... but by default." (National Children's Bureau)

"A good number of discharge processes (according to both families and social workers) occurred without the active involvement of the social worker... (In general), the process of leaving care was not accorded much attention by most social workers." (Marsh & Fisher)

4) <u>Family links are seldom given much consideration. As a result, circumstantial barriers to access may go unrecognised and little practical help is offered to encourage parents' visits. When links wither, chances of the child's return home are diminished.</u>

"Parent-child contact was not a feature relayed by social workers as of importance in relation to placement... Although in the majority of cases parental contact was not being discouraged, the stance was being adopted of waiting and seeing what the parents did... Social workers invariably

commented that they left this (visiting arrangements) to be worked out between the foster parents and the parent.'' (National Children's Bureau)

"Only two sets of parents said their social workers had actually <u>helped</u> them over visiting.'' (Packman)

"The propensity of many placements to frustrate links...often passes quite unrecognised by social workers.'' (Dartington)

In the Dartington cohort, only 36% of families had <u>specific</u> restrictions imposed on their access, but 66% experienced <u>non-specific</u> barriers of distance, travel problems, rules about visits, unwelcoming attitudes etc. At the two year stage, 41 of the 170 children still in care had a mother who did not know their address.

"Even after controlling for other variables, we find that a weakening of parental links is strongly associated with declining chances for the child of returning home. Naturally parental links are not a sufficient condition to ensure exit from care...(but they are) a necessary condition for exit.'' (Dartington)

"We were frequently dismayed and sometimes angered by the way in which social workers so often failed to provide the necessary support and encouragement to maintain visiting. Sometimes they actually seemed to set up 'no win' situations for natural parents, first discouraging visits 'to let the children settle' and later saying that after such a long gap renewed visiting would be upsetting. But this was by no means the whole story. We found that ambivalence towards visiting seemed to be a prevalent attitude in natural parents and foster children as well as in social workers and foster parents. Everyone seemed to draw back from the pain and potential conflict involved.'' (Rowe)

5) <u>Difficulties in maintaining links are exacerbated for both children and social workers by the rapidity with which the families of children in care change and re-constitute themselves.</u>

At the six month follow up, *"The families of no less than one in seven of the children were no longer headed by the same parent figures as they had been six months before.''* (Packman)

"A large proportion of the children came from families with a complex and impermanent structure, often with a mix of different parent figures for each child...Only 27% were 'normal' two parent families...Many families underwent periodic changes of structure with irregular but frequent arrivals and departures of parent figures.'' (Marsh & Fisher)

"Many of these family structures underwent radical changes during the child's absence, even though the stay in care was short...By six months, nearly half of the children will have had a major change in their family structure...These oscillations are most noticeable among the families of younger children, a factor which not only prevents their return home and affects their wider relationships but also greatly hinders contact between parents and children.'' (Dartington)

6) <u>Parents of children in care may feel pushed aside and disillusioned.</u>

"At present many parents seem to feel totally devalued. 'They just don't care about us' was an all too frequent comment...It was clear from many records that natural parents had been allowed — almost encouraged — to lose contact with the department as well as with their children...During the 12 months preceding the study social workers had been in touch with only one-third of the children's 'primary' parents.'' (Rowe)

"Parents felt categorised as the overprotective or rejecting parent...feeling they had to 'prove' to the social worker that their problems were genuinely serious...It was difficult to avoid the impression that psychological theories of family dynamics were often being uncritically applied, with the result that clients were pigeonholed as impossible to work with." (Marsh & Fisher)

"A feeling of helplessness was also engendered by many parents' ignorance and confusion about the law, about official procedures and sometimes the language of law and social work." (Packman)

"Eventually, parents' sense of violation and powerlessness encourages passivity and assumed indifference. However skilled the social worker may be, this is an extremely difficult situation in which to assess parents' long-term viability to care...Parents feel unwanted and that they have nothing more to contribute to the well-being of their children. This feeling increases after time. As contact with the social worker declines, the children settle down and inertia steals over the child care scene, parents feel abandoned and angry." (Dartington)

7) <u>Tension and misunderstandings are often caused by differing values and attitudes to child rearing held by parents, social workers and residential staff.</u>

"The evaluations of parents focussed on the extent to which the care their child was receiving corresponded to a pre-existing framework about appropriate ways of dealing with children...Social work intervention was apt to miss the importance of discipline in the eyes of the parents...These discrepancies (in perception of the purpose of care and of the parents' continued sense of responsibility), were rooted in different concepts of appropriate parenting and were to have long-term consequences for the children's experiences of care and for the parents' acceptance of care as an appropriate solution to their difficulties." (Marsh & Fisher)

Parents usually perceived all types of residential care as being entirely too lax and permissive and feared their children were being 'contaminated'. *"Their reaction was overwhelmingly one of disappointment that the staff seemed unprepared to tackle the children in ways of which they approved."* (Marsh & Fisher)

"Despite some areas of agreement with their fieldwork colleagues, residential social workers tended to operate from an entirely different perspective and set of priorities." (Marsh & Fisher)

8) <u>When parents felt that their problems and wishes were understood, they valued this highly.</u>

"A majority — approaching two-thirds — expressed at least some measure of satisfaction. They reckoned that the social workers had shared their own perceptions of the 'problem' at least in part, and had responded to some, if not all, of what the parents wanted." (Packman)

"Some families...were outstandingly positive about their field social worker...These cases were notable for the convergence of social worker and family understanding of the family's situation." (Marsh & Fisher)

Rowe quotes a mother as saying: *"She was all right, her. She didn't seem like a social worker, more like one of us. I could ask her questions and I'd get an answer, a straight answer."*

9) Overall outcomes may be quite positive in spite of deficiencies in the care system, but evaluation is difficult and for some children the outlook is bleak.

"At follow-up at 6 months it was found that for both groups (those admitted to care and those who were not), basic living conditions were unchanged, health problems were still prominent. When family relationships and parenting standards had changed, it was usually for the better whether the children had been admitted or not. Reports of difficult child behaviour had subsided dramatically." (Packman)

"Overall, about a third of parents were well satisfied with the help they had received; a third had more mixed or neutral feelings and a third were dissatisfied." (Packman)

"Throughout this research report it has been necessary to make critical comments about many aspects of long-term foster care as they were revealed in the children and families we studied. We also report on many cases where the placement has been highly successful in terms of the child's welfare and happiness. We have to conclude that the verdict on long-term fostering is 'not proven'. In spite of many positive aspects, too many of the study placements had drifted from being short-term or indefinite into an undeclared permanency. Too often the children had neither true security nor access to knowledge of their origins. Work with natural parents was seriously deficient and, though foster parents were reasonably content with the support they received, social work input did not seem as effective as one would wish it to be. It was our very strong impression that, although many of the placements we studied were working well, they were doing so in spite of the system rather than because of it." (Rowe)

"Most of the parents and children involved in our study looked back on care with some positive views. Even those parents who described to us their eventual view of care as unacceptable, nonetheless commented on some positive effects on their child's behaviour. (Marsh & Fisher)

"If the processes as described in this study characterise all of the local authorities in England and Wales, and there is every indication that they do, then we can conclude that as many as 7,000 out of the 40,000 children who enter care each year...are destined for a long stay and withering links with their parents and wider family. It also means that at any one time in state care, at least 18,000 children are without meaningful contact with their parents or wider family, a situation which is likely to impair their functioning and increase their social isolation. Sadly, 7,000 of these children are not only isolated but also do not enjoy a stable, alternative care placement and a third of this latter group are likely to be under the age of eleven." (Dartington)

C) Practice Issues & Policy Problems

1) Assessment, recording and knowledge of family history

(Assessments) *"accurately reflected the facts of each family situation and also shared some parental perceptions of what the problems were. Where they were sometimes weak was in their exploration of kin and neighbourhood networks as potential sources of help; and in their recognition of the strengths and positives within families...A wider perspective is sometimes needed which avoids an exclusively problem-focussed approach."* (Packman)

"It has to be said that almost without exception, the case records were seriously inadequate as a source of basic data on natural parents and

practically never contained a systematic account of the whole family's situation, problems and strengths even at the time of admission. (As a result) *"many records could not provide a really satisfactory basis for future work with either child or family."* (Rowe)

"Residential social workers were frequently extremely poorly informed on the child's background, the reasons for care and its purposes. The history of the family's difficulties, whom parents turned to for help, and what approaches had been tried and abandoned were as absent from the residential social worker's account of the case as from the fieldworker's." (Marsh & Fisher)

"The paucity of information held by most (long-term) foster parents was most striking...Moreover, when we asked whether they thought the child knew these things, it became clear that they had not passed on even the meagre store that they had." (Rowe)

"Many (court) reports can be severely criticised, particularly with reference to the criteria normally applied to reports from other experts and professionals." (Hilgendorf)

(During court hearings) *"we observed that social workers often had difficulty in finding information. This particularly applied to details of decision making, of meetings between parents and children and of contact between social worker and parents."* (Adcock & White)

2) Social workers appear to lack time and skills for direct work with children.

"There was little evidence to suggest that social workers were much involved in direct contact with children...The child's primary carers, foster parents and residential staff were seen to have greater opportunities. Where skills beyond this were required, the social worker generally referred the case to an acknowledged specialist in child development, health or education." (National Children's Bureau)

"Many social workers feel that they should make a point of seeing foster children on their own at least sometimes. Nearly two-thirds of our social workers reported that they had seen the child alone in the past year...(but it seemed that) 'seeing alone' was often very brief and passed unnoticed by child and foster parent." (Rowe)

"At two years, nearly half the children were receiving visits from social workers at less than monthly intervals." (Dartington)

3) Reviews and case conferences are not central to the decision making process.

"It would seem clear that reviews at present do not play a vital part in developing and monitoring long-term plans for children." (Sinclair and Webb)

"Broadly speaking, reviews were rarely seen...as taking decisions or formulating plans but rather as part of an administrative procedure — a statutory requirement...In our experience it was unusual for natural parents, child or foster parents to be present." (National Children's Bureau)

"The discussions sought confirmation of existing care plans rather than consideration of fresh initiatives." (Dartington)

"Social workers were confident that the full number of reviews had been carried out in only 35% of cases." (Adcock & White)

"Although case conferences usually had a problem orientation, the lack of clarity of their executive responsibility meant that often social workers would use them as vehicles for ratifying plans which had already been formulated." (National Children's Bureau)

4) Supervision

Only the National Children's Bureau examined supervision of social workers and its place in decision making, though Adcock & White made some enquiries and found that nearly one social worker in five was dissatisfied with the supervision received. The Bureau report states:

"Our experience of practice (in 11 authorities) was that with only a few notable exceptions, supervision sessions did not occur at the departmentally prescribed frequency and that overall their content did not correspond to our understanding of what supervision entailed."

"Overall planning for a case was not a routine consideration of the supervision session. Cases were rarely selected systematically and discussed."

"The initiative for planning...rested with the social worker with little by way of support in this process coming from the supervision session unless directly raised by the social worker."

5) Child care policies have only a limited effect on practice

Policies — as distinct from procedures — appear to be little known by field social workers. Packman paid considerable attention to trying to determine their effectiveness but found them hard to define.

"Looking from the top downwards in our sample departments, official policy statements were generally fragmented, partial and sometimes elusive and of uncertain status...Looking from the bottom up, the sense of confusion and ambiguity is intensified. In the social workers' eyes policy is not always acknowledged or recognised and its links with practice on a case by case basis are frequently obscure." (Packman)

"Except when stated in the broadest and most abstract terms, child care policies do not command a consensus of support." (Packman)

"Despite the excellence of the non-accidental injury handbooks, we found that in many social work offices copies were not available." (Hilgendorf)

III   Themes & Reasons

As the researchers analysed their findings, pondered and worked over them and sought explanations, various themes clearly emerged. Of course they are not all equally emphasised in every report but all are common to more than one. It is these themes — which form the flesh of our apple — which contain crucial messages for all concerned with the child care service. They are of greater importance than the specific findings because they begin to provide explanations about how and why deficiencies in practice occur in spite of so much effort and goodwill. The themes most relevant to issues about social work decisions are:

1)   Social workers' pessimism about care

2)   Care and prevention

3) Care is not a unitary concept

4) Problems over values and expectations

5) The paradox of social workers' power and passivity

6) The tension between professionalism and bureaucracies

7) The key role of team leaders

8) Issues of compulsion and control

9) Attitudes to the natural family

10) What clients value in social workers

It seems best to consider each theme in turn before moving on to examine the core of the apple, the implications and the researchers' recommendations.

1) Pessimism about care

Virtually all social workers appear to view admission to care very negatively. They see it as a last resort and as a sign of failure to prevent the break up of families. They are also worried about what the care experience will do to children and parents. Residential care is looked on with special pessimism. This attitude only serves to increase the stigma, shame, depression and passivity in families, field and residential social workers alike. It hampers proper planning because social workers close their eyes to the possibility of admission and keep hoping that it will not have to happen. When the crisis comes, no-one is adequately prepared.

The emphasis on whether or not to admit seems to have got out of focus. It draws attention away from consideration of children's needs and how to meet them. An over-emphasis on admission may actually hamper the search for other options as well as inhibiting the creative use of care for some children in some circumstances. Indeed there seems to be a profound ambiguity between seeing care as a service to which families and children are entitled and policies which strive to keep children out of care *at all costs*. Whereas those with money buy shared care for their children almost as a matter of course, those without means either have shared care withheld (because being 'in care' is bad) or it is imposed — perhaps for ever. There is certainly evidence from these research studies which confirms the impression of care as all too often insecure and unstable and not resolving the problems which led to care in the first place. However, extreme pessimism about care is unwarranted and damaging. The research shows that the majority of children and families felt that it had achieved some benefits for them and those who asked for care and were refused were apt to feel bitter, desperate and unhelped.

2) Care and prevention

None of these research studies was specifically concerned with prevention. Nevertheless, both directly and indirectly the researchers stress the importance of preventive services. They see these as crucial in avoiding the need for admission and there is evidence from Packman's study in particular that alternatives such as day care do help to reduce the need for full-time care.

But the researchers also refer to the potentialities of using short-term care as a means of preventing the permanent break-up of families by offering temporarily relief. By implication, they point out that if care is to be used positively and beneficially, it has to be one of a range of options and used as part of a plan. Admission should have a purpose and not be just a last resort, and work with child and family after admission has to be focussed on achieving the plan.

A further theme related to prevention is the need to strengthen social workers' professional confidence to resist pressure for inappropriate admissions.

Mention has already been made of the finding that powerful pressure from agencies such as the police, courts and schools may propel into care youngsters who probably will not benefit. This pressure can only be resisted by clear and firm explanations of professional values and policies and by having alternative strategies to offer.

3) Care is not a unitary concept

It is noteworthy that in central and local government papers, reports and policy documents, in the general press and even in social work writing, care is more often than not referred to as though it provided a similar, standardised experience and as though it were being used for similar reasons for all children. By contrast, both the Packman and National Children's Bureau studies found it necessary to differentiate on the basis of the reason for admission. The NCB separated 'family service' from interventions based on the need to 'rescue' the child or to protect others from the child's behaviour. Packman named three groups of children 'victims', 'villains' and 'volunteered'. (The 'volunteered' are the equivalent of the NCB 'family service' cases.)

The purposes of admission — as well as the reasons for it — are likely to be different for each of these groups and it is clearly quite inappropriate to think that policies and practices suitable for neglected babies are likely to be suitable for delinquent adolescents. Nor can one equate the care experience of a child who spends six weeks in an observation and assessment centre and then returns home with that of a child who spends sixteen years in a foster home or a young person who spends four or five years in a residential establishment.

The need for greater clarity about the purposes of care and for plans and practices to be based on and supportive of these purposes is a recurring theme coming up both directly and indirectly in virtually all the studies.

4) Values, expectations and mutual understanding

Concern about the gulf between the values and expectations of social workers and their clients and about problems of communication between them runs throughout the reports. Researchers' anxieties about values surface in relation to various aspects but above all over issues surrounding the reasons for and purposes of admission to care.

Social work judgements often appear to take the form of implicit assumptions e.g. care is the last resort; fostering is best for young children; residential care is appropriate for adolescents. Values based on class/cultural upbringing, on professional training, on life experience, on departmental policy etc., are generally not made explicit or consciously weighed up in spite of the major differences that exist.

Marsh's study in particular shows the clash of values over discipline. It shows social workers vainly attempting to get parents to examine and modify attitudes and relationships, and parents striving — also vainly — to get across their concern about their child's behaviour and their own need to exert what they consider to be responsible authority. The other studies also provide vivid and disturbing examples of conflicting perceptions with parents and social workers pulling in opposite directions and the child caught in the middle. Some of these have been highlighted in the previous section of this paper. It seems that sometimes the differences are unrecognised. Sometimes they are known, but open discussion and clarification are avoided because of the pain and anger involved.

Professional ideology over issues, such as child protection or family rights, evidently plays an important part in social workers' decisions. It may, unfortunately, take the place of knowledge. These are not the only research reports to draw attention to the lack of reference to theories of social work practice or child development when social workers are explaining their decisions. For some of the researchers this raised serious questions about the knowledge and skills base of social work and led them to wonder about the way knowledge is used — or, more often, not used.

5) Power and passivity — a paradox

The power that social workers wield is explicitly commented on by some researchers and is implicit in the findings of others. Yet there is a curious paradox here. Far from considering themselves to be powerful, the field social workers interviewed in these research studies evidently felt themselves to be power*less* and 'at the bottom of the heap' in the hierarchy. They felt they were lacking in resources, in the hands of courts and other outside agencies and battered by clients' needs and demands.

Established social work methods have always depended largely on surveillance and the containment of problems (no doubt because cure and change are so difficult) and the prevailing stance is still re-active rather than pro-active. Although these points have been made before, these researchers were clearly taken aback by what they describe as the passivity of social workers with 'wait and see' the most usual 'plan'. Clearly there are dilemmas and difficult balances to be struck. Client self-determination and social workers' wish not to impose their own values are important. It is by no means certain that a more interventionist stance would be either appropriate or possible — especially in the early weeks after a child's admission. Many useful initiatives may be precluded by lack of time. Yet the prevailing picture of drift, passivity and lack of planning is pervasive and clearly not conducive to child welfare. A member of the practitioners' group described the sense of drift as 'startling'.

6) The tension between professionalism and bureaucracies

There is an inherent — and perhaps inevitable — tension created by the effort to provide an individualised service in a large bureaucracy. The researchers were very aware of this and prevalent in several of their reports is the notion of the social worker as a 'street level bureaucrat' struggling to cope simultaneously with the public's demands and expectations and the agency's limited resources and uncertain policies.

Problems of working within 'the system' come to the fore in the researchers' discussions of decision making as do the difficulties of obtaining the resources that the child or family may need. 'Working the system' — for example to obtain a residential place — may over-ride other aspects and lead to a particular legal route which, in other respects, goes counter to professional judgement.

Another theme linked to this is the problem for a bureaucracy in acting as a good parent. The inevitable splitting of day to day and overall responsibility, the changes of placement or of social worker imposed by administrative requirements, the lack of any individual — other than the current caretaker and social worker — who feels a personal sense of responsibility for the child's future, are all features of child care in social services departments.

The tension between professionalism and bureaucracy shows up also in the problems for senior managers over developing policies which can and will be put into practice by fieldworkers, which are clear and effective and yet sufficiently flexible to allow for professional discretion in individual circumstances. To work well, policies should include specific strategies to deal with different groups of children and must avoid blanket assertions. Some degree of flexibility is essential. Policies need to be discussed at all levels in the department so that they become accepted and 'usable' within the department, in negotiation with outside agencies and in discussion with clients. This has to be a continuous process with regular up-dating. Policies which are global, which are not well known or which seem only concerned with financial savings will not be effective. At present there seems rather little connection between policy and decisions on individual cases.

7) The key role of team leaders/supervisors

Some of the deficiencies in the current supervision of social workers which were disclosed in the National Children's Bureau study, have already been mentioned in the previous section on findings. But the key role of supervisor/team leader was a theme that emerged in several other reports in which researchers lamented the apparent ineffectiveness of supervisors or team leaders in achieving better planning or offering the kind of support which would enable social workers to get alongside clients' grief, pain and loneliness and stay with them through it. Supervision, as seen in these studies, did not seem to offer either real support or appropriate control.

Current moves to turn supervisors into 'team managers' may help to achieve control, but offer little hope of the more effective support which is vital to improving practice. Indeed, these moves may be another indication of management's apparent failure to appreciate the levels of stress which fieldworkers experience in working face to face with clients.

8) Issues of compulsion and control

The theme of control, its use, value and dangers is clearly central to any discussion of decision making even though there is a danger of equating decision making with power. The research findings on the negative effects of many place of safety orders and other compulsory measures have already been mentioned, but there is also the crucial issue of *why* compulsion is increasing and *how* it is — or should be — related to good planning.

The desire to find a better balance between children's needs and parents' wishes and rights led to the introduction in the Children Act 1975 of new powers for local authorities to assume parental rights and duties. The research reports of Stevenson, Adcock and White and Rowe show that in general these powers have been used responsibly and appropriately. Yet the Dartington and Packman studies make it plain that in relation to some other measures (e.g. care procedures and Place of Safety Orders), all is not well as regards control and compulsion.

It is noteworthy that compulsion is against most social workers' ethos, although it is increasingly being used. The idea seems to be to 'get control in order to plan and safeguard'. Yet constructive planning seems all too often absent. There are suggestions in the research that control is being confused with planning and that in a laudable desire to manage risk, to improve decision making, to avoid drift and be 'firmer', controls are imposed at a time and in a manner that is unconstructive and often counter-productive.One reason for this may have been the lack of any soundly based and agreed theory about when compulsion or voluntary care is the best route. These research studies may now provide the impetus to develop a clear professional philosophy based on research evidence.

9) Attitudes to the natural family

The devaluing of parents and relatives and their potential contribution to the care and well-being of their children is a hang-over from an era of child rescue and the belief in a fresh start away from contaminating influences. It provides a prime example of conflicting values. It is ironic that the Marsh research should now demonstrate that many parents feel that their children are being contaminated by residential care!

Serious failures in the delivery of services to parents of children in care have been noted by American researchers in recent years and also found in these British studies. Lack of practical resources and the harsh realities of how little social workers can do in face of financial hardship, bad housing and environmental degradation are, inevitably, recurring themes. But, more usefully, these research studies shed light on areas in which improvements in practice do not depend on practical resources or on other agencies. The need to consult, inform and work *with* parents; the value of enlisting the help of the wider family whenever possible; the importance of recognising and understanding parents' response to separation; all these are suggestions which have immediate potential for improving practice.

10) Social worker characteristics which clients value

All the research projects which included interviews with parents report similar messages from them. What was appreciated most was honesty, naturalness and reliability along with an ability to listen. Clients appreciated being kept informed, having their feelings understood, having the stress of parenthood accepted and getting practical help as well as moral support. The social workers whose assistance was valued had a capacity to help parents retain their role as responsible, authority figures in relation to their children. These workers were actively involved in the processes, negotiations and family dynamics of admission and discharge. When these qualities were present, social work help was highly valued.

IV The Core of the Apple

This brings us to the really basic issues — the core of the apple. WHY is there still such a gulf between hopes and actualities in our child care services? What fundamental lessons can be deduced from these various research reports?

Six main messages come through:

1) The depth, complexity and long-standing nature of child care problems makes them fiendishly difficult to deal with, whatever one's level of knowledge, experience and competence. Yet the main responsibility rests with those on the lowest rung of the hierarchy who usually lack the seniority and power to gain access to key resources.

2) At present the system tends to constrain rather than support and 'caring for the carers' receives little attention in social services departments. As a member of the practitioners' working party pointed out, managers deal with problems, but social workers cope with pain and are left to cope after managers have moved on to the next problem.

As these research reports show, there is also a lack of well thought-out, relevant policies which would provide a general framework of support. At the level of the individual case, neither supervision nor the review and case conference system seem to offer appropriate direction and support for fieldworkers.

3) Our huge, bureaucratic structures make it difficult to provide good enough parenting for the individual child in care. Reading the research, one has the impression of lumbering, elephantine systems that are difficult to handle and slow to respond. When they do respond, they tend to lurch first in one direction and then in the opposite one as management strives to keep on course. Much of this is not unique to child care but typical of most large organisations. But there are few equivalents to the way in which a system (the social services department) holds such awesome and total power over an individual (the child in care).

4) It seems very apparent that the deep emotional problems generated by the separation/care experience receive insufficient attention (parents feel ignored and direct work with children is minimal). It is not clear whether the pain and

grief goes unrecognised or whether it is recognised but social workers shut their eyes to it because, lacking support themselves, they cannot tolerate the pain of getting involved and working with feelings.

It could be that, wittingly or unwittingly, bureaucratic arrangements serve to ensure that field and residential staff do not become too involved and are not allowed to offer too personal or individualised a service for fear that it will get out of control. There are also some indications that social workers may use their power to avoid pain e.g. it is in some ways 'easier' to get and use a Place of Safety Order than to discuss and negotiate with parents to achieve secure but voluntary care.

5)   There is no adequate, comprehensive research, practice, or value base which would help practitioners to decide when admission to care would be appropriate and for which groups of children. There has been virtually no monitoring of outcomes and child care lacks even the level of research attention given to delinquency. We urgently need to know more about when and under what conditions aims are more likely to be met by admission to care or by the use of continued preventive services in the community. We may be going to 'reap the whirlwind' in a few years time from having kept children out of care 'at all costs'.

6)   There is an overwhelming impression of social workers' passivity and their feelings of helplessness and being at the mercy of events and actions of other people and other agencies. Part of this can probably be attributed to a tradition of containing and responding rather than taking initiatives and to the feeling of defensiveness generated by over-large caseloads and 'bombardment'. But the combined messages from these nine research studies do seem to be that social workers and their seniors are not offered the opportunity to acquire the sophisticated skills, knowledge and qualitative experience to equip them to deal confidently with the complex and extremely emotive issues raised by work with children and families.

The deficiencies in assessment and in family history taking which were disclosed in the research provide a useful example of this, for they are surely not due *just* to shortage of time, relevant though this may be. One is faced with the inescapable conclusion that too many social workers are not enabled to acquire nor encouraged to use the necessary skills. The result is that the whole basis for planning is shaky. Decisions are made on inadequate evidence and it is not surprising if goals are unclear or if there is a lack of congruence between goals and what is actually done — or not done. (This is what Marsh and Fisher call a general lack of a model of practice that clarifies and links goals and inputs.)

It is not surprising — even if depressing — to discover these deficiencies. We have known for a long while that a two year training is a quite inadequate time in which to obtain the necessary knowledge and acquire the essential skills. Students are exposed to a wide range of theories and make a start on developing their techniques, but before these can be properly absorbed and become 'usable', the student becomes a practitioner and is pitchforked into the stressful arena of an area office where local traditions, attitudes and work habits soon push out the rather tenuously grasped knowledge obtained on the course. Subsequent in-service training, conferences and seminars are usually brief and do not contain any element of practical work. Thus, while people may have considerably more knowledge than they are able to demonstrate in their work, too often they do not 'know' in a way that makes them feel like confident professionals.

V Implications

The implications of these research studies are profound and far reaching. Some of the changes needed are major and will require long-term effort; others could be achieved relatively easily. It seems important to consider both problems and recommendations in context so that appropriate strategies can be devised.

Some of the difficulties which beset social services departments are beyond their power to change. For instance, much of the pressure comes from social and economic factors over which they have no control. Some organisational stresses are inherent in large local government departments. No amount of re-structuring of the service or increased knowledge in social workers is going to lessen the intractability of some clients' long standing problems or remove the stress of dealing with them. But in spite of these very real limitations, a great deal could be achieved if the lessons of the research were to be heeded.

Some of the necessary improvements in training, including post-qualifying training opportunities for all would, of course, have major resource implications. But even within the present budgets something could be done both in training establishments and on in-service courses to improve knowledge of child development and child care law. And given motivation, support and encouragement, even busy practitioners can improve their existing skills and can learn and apply new ones.

Within our present social services departments is a reservoir of knowledge, skill and experience that somehow has to be re-directed and made more available to clients and to those who provide the direct services to them. It might take a revolution in managerial thinking, but the primary constraints are not financial.

Some of the most urgent needs appear to be shifts in attitude and priorities, increased understanding, more sensitive perception of clients' feelings by social workers and of social workers' feelings by managers. Many of these have already been mentioned in this paper, others are to be found in each of the research reports that have been reviewed here which also contain a variety of practical suggestions. The situation is undoubtedly serious because the gap between aims and achievements in the child care service is still distressingly wide. A major effort is clearly required. But it is encouraging that so many of the necessary changes are achievable given the will on the part of all concerned.

PART II   Short Summaries of the Research

The following summaries were prepared by the research authors themselves, sometimes before the publication of their reports.

In addition there is a table giving information about each project on sample size, methods of data collection used and topics covered.

Who needs care?
Social work decisions about children.
Jean Packman, John Randall and Nicola Jacques
Blackwell — Spring 1986.

This study explored the basis, process and outcomes of decisions for or against the admission of children to care in two similar local authorities in the South of England. All cases considered for care in one year were monitored and then followed up six months later. Social workers and parents of the children concerned were interviewed, in addition to other social services and extra-departmental personnel.

Some of the major points of interest to emerge were as follows:

Most children considered came from the poorest and most deprived sector of the population, where material handicaps created and compounded problems of relationships and behaviour.

There were no sharply identifiable differences between the children admitted to care, and those not, though the admitted children tended to have somewhat more severe relationship and behaviour problems, or there were more extreme difficulties with parental behaviour.

Admission to care had several different purposes and the characteristics of children, families and the legal route of entry used reflected this. It provided a child care service for families in difficulty; a rescue service for children at risk; and a 'care and control' service for troublesome children. The first of these functions has been losing ground to the other two.

Although child and family characteristics matched these different functions there was considerable overlap and departmental responses varied. Willingness to admit at all, to use the courts and compulsion, or the voluntary alternative, and to respond more readily to some types of case rather than others, varied between the two authorities studied. Practice in the two authorities varied most in relation to troublesome teenagers and to children at risk of neglect and ill-treatment. Resources to support such responses were also unevenly distributed: day care for the under fives and residential care for all age groups being striking examples.

Field social workers played a central role in admission decisions despite different departmental procedures. They carried considerable and necessary discretion. However, they often lacked clear and detailed policy guidance to support that discretion. Departmental policies were often imprecise, ambiguous and poorly disseminated, and established structures for the discussion, development and challenge of policies need to be encouraged.

Admission to care as a 'last resort' is a popular stance which was sometimes found to be unhelpful, contributing to ill-planned, traumatic admissions and unstable placements; it also ignores the fact that some admissions were experienced as helpful. In addition, some 'prevention' that is little more than saying 'no' to an admission was experienced as neglectful and profoundly *unhelpful* by the families concerned.

Compulsory admissions were clearly more problematic than voluntary care. Admissions were less well planned and executed; parental reactions were often hostile; time spent in care was, on average, more lengthy; and there was no *short-term* evidence that planning for the children was any better. There was also evidence of widespread use of Place of Safety Orders (by Police as well as social workers) some of which went unrecorded in central government statistics. The worst aspects of compulsion often characterised these Orders. The present trend towards more compulsory and fewer voluntary admissions therefore seems unfortunate.

Children lost in care
The family contact of children in care.
Spencer Millham, Roger Bullock, Ken Hosie and
Martin Haak.
Gower — Autumn 1985

Between 1980 and 1983, the Dartington Social Research Unit studied 450 children entering local authority care and the problems some experienced in maintaining links with their families. Over a two year period, the care careers of all children were traced whatever their age, status or duration in care. The experiences of families, children, care givers and social workers negotiating the care experience were scrutinised. The research concludes:

— If a child remains in local authority care for longer than five weeks, it has a very strong chance (two out of three cases) of still being in care two years later;

— The maintenance of close contact with their families is the best indicator that a child will leave local authority care rapidly;

— Children and adolescents, even if their chances of returning home are slim, function better psychologically, socially and educationally if they remain in regular contact with their families.

The conflict between nurturing the 'blood tie' versus the child's need for 'psychological parenting' affects very few children entering care. Most who linger long in care are adolescents with well-forged family links, these they wish and ought to maintain, because it is to the family or its neighbourhood that young people will return.

The importance of encouraging family links is further emphasized by the frequency of transfer and movement between the care placements of children, both those in fostering and residential care. For example, at the end of two years, half of the children who are still in care will have had one or more precipitate changes of placement. This rather than change of social worker means that the child's family, however inadequate, may be the only enduring feature in many children's lives. For some children, stable care situations are very difficult to achieve.

The study also makes it clear that the turbulent, rapidly changing households from which children come, act as a significant barrier to contact between parents and children. In addition to parents' preoccupation with change, social workers have many pressing demands on their time and, with limited resources, find it difficult to keep track of family changes and to offer sufficiently flexible support.

Unfortunately, social workers take a rather limited view of the importance of maintaining links between parent and child. Contacts are left to 'emerge', consequent upon other social work decisions. In addition, the wider family which often exists locally, and separated fathers, are rarely incorporated into social work thinking about support for the child and ongoing contact.

As a result, at the outset of their entry to care, nearly three-quarters of the 450 children studied found great difficulty in maintaining contact with their parents. The barriers they faced were of two kinds: *specific restrictions,* which are usually placed by social workers on the access of individuals and which affected one-third of the children on entry, and *non-specific restrictions*, that is barriers inherent in placements, such as distance or routine, and which affected two-thirds of the children on entry. About a quarter of all of the children were affected by both sorts of restrictions on contact with home.

As time passed, specific restrictions on parents' access to children actually increased, often to help maintain placements in difficulty, although the disruptive potential of visiting parents was greatly over-estimated by social workers. Restrictions on contact were not sufficiently scrutinised and were allowed to linger after the initial reasons for their application had evaporated. In addition, non-specific barriers to contact, that is in the distance, routine, rules and inaccessibility of placements, remained pressing throughout the child's care experiences.

Social workers' visits to parents, children and care givers decline over time. By the end of two years, one-third of mothers, four-fifths of fathers and nearly half of the children in care were receiving infrequent visits. Unfortunately, parents need encouragement to maintain contact with their child and to feel that they can contribute; without social workers urging them to keep in contact, many fall by the wayside. It is not that social workers dismiss the importance of links with families but that the ongoing needs of tranquil care situations are often displaced by the succession of crises presented to social workers by other families.

At the end of two years, 170 children (38%) of the original 450 entries to care still remained the responsibility of Social Services, although a quarter of these children were living at home 'on trial'. About four-fifths of children still absent in care were experiencing severe barriers to maintaining contact with their parents, nearly half had restrictions still imposed on a specific adult and almost all endured pressing non-specific barriers to contact.

Fifty-four of the 170 children who remained in care had no contact with mother or father, siblings or the wider family at the end of two years. A third of these children were likely to stay in care for the foreseeable future. Thus, two-fifths of all the long-stay children, that is being in care for three years or more, had lost contact with their parents by the time two years had elapsed, yet there were no social work reasons for the exclusion of the natural family in two-thirds of the cases. The implications of this nationally are that at any one time in state care, at least 18,000 children are likely to be without meaningful contact with their parents or with their wider family, a situation that is likely to impair their functioning and increase their general social isolation. Further, 7,000 of these children are not only isolated but also do not enjoy a stable, alternative care placement and a third of this latter group are likely to be under the age of 11.

While parental and/or children's indifference contributes to this situation, it is also clear from this study that much child isolation is due to the care process itself and the failure to accord the maintenance of links between parent and absent child the priority it merits. However, improvements are discernible. These can be seen in the recent access legislation, the provision of codes of practice regarding parental contact and an increasing awareness in Social Services Departments of the complexity of 'belonging' for separated children, a complexity which the study amply demonstrates. In addition, the maintenance of parental links, while time-consuming, is a priority which accords well with the training social workers have received, the ideology of the profession and, unlike many intractable family problems, is a task well within the scope of present social work arrangements.

The research has also explored the factors affecting children's length of stay in care, their educational experience, the care careers of juvenile offenders (Section 7(7) 1969 CYPA) and the consequences of remanding children to care in terms of their court disposals.

In care: a study of social work decision making
Jeni Vernon and David Fruin
NCB — Autumn 1985.

The aim of the study was to examine social work decision-making and its relationship to the length of time children spend in care. Key events in children's care careers were examined as well as how social workers make plans for their child clients. The research was carried out in 11 English local authorities and took the form of following case histories of 185 children (of varying ages and length of time in care, approximately half of whom were followed from their point of entry to the care system) for a period of not less than one year.

The study found that the key personnel in taking decisions about children in care were the main grade social workers. They admitted children to care very reluctantly and often only after long and sustained pressure from other agencies or even the child's family. Children were admitted to care in varying circumstances which were found to have implications for the length of time they remained in care. Admissions of children under 11 could be divided between those providing a *family service* and those requiring *intervention*. The former occurred when there was a family crisis of some kind which was expected to be temporary and usually resulted in a short stay in care. Intervention for the under 11s occurred when the social workers felt there was a risk to the child. With the over 11s, admission was much more likely to occur as a response to the child's behaviour as opposed to family circumstances.

Seventy of the 185 children in the sample had left care during the study period, the majority of them returning to their families. Many children left care with little or no involvement of the social worker, particularly when the admission had been to provide a service to the family. Where the social worker was active in the process of discharge this was usually as a response to pressure from the parents or child or because a placement had broken down, rather than at the initiative of the social worker on the basis of the child's interests or needs. Paradoxically, the actions of parents were often significant factors in whether children returned home from care, yet in many cases social workers did not work with the parents to achieve this end.

The study found that social workers did not actively plan what should happen to children once they came into care. Plans emerged over time in response to a variety of factors in the child's overall situation. Given the complex circumstances of many children in care, social workers tended to adopt a 'wait and see' policy. In assessing what is happening, what is likely to happen and what they think should happen, their stance is intended to be neutral. But this stance implicitly denies the potential influence of their actions and results in their behaviour being both passive and reactive.

The study found that formal venues for decision-making like reviews or case conferences did not contribute significantly to planning a child's future. One third of reviews were form-filling activities only and involved no discussion with other staff, parents or children. Even when meetings were held, these reviews usually focussed on what had happened in the past and did not involve looking forward.

In and Out of Care — The experience of children, parents and social workers
Fisher, M.; Marsh, P.; Phillips, D. with
Sainsbury, E. E.
Batsford/BAAF 1986

This Sheffield University client study was part of a programme of E.S.R.C. research into children in care. It describes the experiences of workers and clients at admission to care, movements within care, and discharge from care. Up to five participants in each case were interviewed in depth at each of these stages and some families were followed through all three stages over a period of 18 months. Fieldwork was carried out in 1982 and 1983. 331 interviews were carried out with 61 mothers and 32 fathers of 79 children (aged eight and over) with 14 siblings, alongside the relevant 80 field social workers, 34 residential social workers, 14 foster mothers and 9 foster fathers. In all the cases a comparison of different participants' views was possible. Basic family and child care career details were analysed for the full population of 350 families from which the sample was drawn. The structure of the research sample effectively excluded black families and children under eight, but included a full range of placement types and children taken and received into care by many different routes.

Findings:

1) Only one quarter of the families had both natural parents present. The families had complex structures which often changed substantially over short periods of time.

2) Arguments within the family were experienced as particularly stressful when family members changed or were absent (e.g. fathers). Most families had a long history of problems and arguments. A relatively common past solution to these problems had been the removal of a child (e.g. to a step parent or to care).

3) The request for care, or parental views of the origin of compulsory care, was linked to a "last straw" event for the parents and sometimes for the child. This was usually relatively minor. Social workers rarely had a full view of the history of problems and solutions; they often did not realise the importance of the "last straw", leaving families with a sense of frustration and inadequacy.

4) Families envisaged that entry into care would mean that children received close control. They assumed that care, even if it arose compulsorily via the courts, was an extension and addition of their own care. This was linked to a view that responsibility for children was permanently carried by the family and, to some degree, by all adults. Social workers, on the other hand, assumed that legal changes in rights and responsibilities signified fundamental changes in the parents' roles. They rarely involved parents in decisions about placements or about the details of the care of the child. Organisational and managerial structures made it difficult for them to do this, especially for residential care. Much of the discussion between social workers and clients about entry to care appeared to be at cross-purposes.

5) Parents often showed relief at the reduction of daily stress when their child entered care (e.g. less arguments or improved relationships with a sibling), they described practical and other difficulties in contacting care staff and

visiting care units (this was less true of fostering). Social workers sometimes misinterpreted this as rejection (especially in the context of confusion over the "last straw", see (3), and cross purposes about changes in roles because of care, see (4)).

6)   Field social workers had a negative view of residential care, seeing it as a last resort and feeling a sense of failure at its use. They rarely shared detailed information with residential units.

7)   Residential workers shared some of the negative views of their work (especially as regards the unstable and impersonal elements of their units). They regretted the lack of joint work with field staff. As care progressed residential staff tended to view the child in similar ways to the parents, whereas field staff became more closely identified with the child's views. Parents themselves were often shadowy figures to both residential and field staff.

8)   Care sometimes developed into an end in itself with little sense of purpose or plan.

9)   Children described care as a process of "wising up" to new rules, as a relief from arguments, as a more liberal regime than home and as inappropriately impersonal (e.g. in lack of interest taken in them and blanket rules and procedures, especially if inappropriate to their age group). After entry to care many children changed all their friends. Few had any doubts about their desire to be home if that was at all possible.

10)   The end of care was often by default e.g. unplanned increases in home visits, impulsive removal by parents, the reaching of age 18. In contrast to entry the social workers did not involve managerial staff or other colleagues.

11)   There was some evidence of problems arising from care e.g. reported high levels of anxiety, irresponsible behaviour from children, and difficulties in reforming families. Despite their criticisms most families seemed satisfied with care, but initial overall expectations had been very low.

12)   A few clients were particularly complimentary about their social workers, especially welcoming a "cards on the table" and a businesslike approach, a consistent showing of concern, and an exhibited desire for their involvement in the decisions and activities of care.

Long Term Foster Care
Jane Rowe, Hilary Cain, Marion Hundleby and
Anne Keane.
Batsford/BAAF — 1984

This is a research study of 'successful' foster placements in that all had lasted for a minimum of three years and the average was nine years. (Placements which had broken down were not included.) Foster children and some natural parents were interviewed as well as social workers and foster parents. Four hundred cases were studied from six local authorities.

The overall picture was encouraging with three out of four foster homes being rated by social workers as providing an 'excellent' or 'good' home for the child. Most of the children were very positive about their foster homes and stressed the importance of having a family, but there were disturbing pockets of unhappiness, fears and worries many of which could have been alleviated by better social work practice.

Problems of behaviour and adjustment were more common among the study children than in the general population or among adopted children, but less frequent than reported in other research on foster children. (Children in this study had been in placement longer.)

This research neither supports nor disproves the theory that parental contact is helpful to long-term foster children. The overall level of visiting was very low with only 11% of children having contact with even one parent as often as three times a year. Children admitted to care over the age of five years were the most likely to remain in contact with parents and relatives. Contact with grandparents appeared to be helpful and presented few problems.

Unless they were still in touch or had clear recollection of contact, most foster children knew remarkably little about their parents and still less about why they were in care. Foster parents had been given little information but often failed to pass on the few facts they had. Many children were curious but found it difficult to ask questions. They particularly wanted to know what their parents looked like.

The delegation of day to day responsibility to foster parents seemed to be working fairly well but contained the seeds of potentially serious confusions eg in only a third of the cases studied were foster parents and social worker agreed about what was supposed to happen over consents to operations.

Contrary to expectations, children fostered by relatives seemed to be doing better in virtually all respects than those fostered by others. Relatives acting as foster parents valued social worker support and fewer than one in five showed any interest in the possibility of custodianship.

In recent years the proportion of new placements involving school aged children has markedly increased but substantial numbers of babies and toddlers are still going into long-term foster homes. There was evidence of some improvement in services to natural parents and more careful planning but little change in attitudes to rehabilitation. Few long-term foster children are expected to return to their natural parents. Interest in adoption by foster parents appeared to have increased.

Part II   31

Decision Making in Statutory Reviews on Children in Care
Ruth Sinclair.
Gower — 1984.

As part of the 'Boarding Out Regulations' local authorities are required regularly to review the cases of all children placed in foster care; the 1969 Children and Young Persons Act requires that the cases of all children under Care Orders to the local authority should be reviewed every six months. However, there is considerable evidence to suggest that statutory reviews are not carried out regularly or comprehensively and hence an opportunity for effective planning and monitoring of child care is wasted.

A detailed study of almost three hundred reviews was undertaken in three social work areas in one local authority. Some of the main findings from this study are presented below, although it has not been possible to draw out fully the implications from these findings in this limited summary.

The organisation of reviews: The conduct of reviews on children in residential homes is very different from that of reviews undertaken in area offices, covering children who are fostered. Of the former, 93% of reviews were held within six months of the previous review; only 81% of the latter were so held. No review in a residential home was less than 11 minutes in length and 20% were longer than 50 minutes; 50% of reviews conducted in area offices lasted 10 minutes or less. The average attendance at residential reviews was 8 people, at area office reviews in only one instance was anyone other than SSD staff present. Children were included in almost 10% of reviews in residential homes; no children or their families were included in area office reviews.

The functions of reviews: Ten possible functions of reviews were identified. Briefly, these were administration, monitoring, supervisory, decision-making, informing superiors, co-ordinating information, increasing specificity, developmental, reassessment, long-term planning. This list was used to assess which functions social workers thought reviews ought to fulfil and which in fact they did fulfil, and which functions the researcher assessed as being fulfilled by each review. Two general conclusions arise from this: reviews are multifunctions; there is considerable disagreement among social services staff over the most appropriate functions of reviews. The administrative, information exchange and monitoring functions were more in evidence in area office reviews than were functions associated with decision-making or planning; there was much greater emphasis in residential reviews on decision-making and much less on administrative or supervisory activity. These differences together with the lack of consensus among staff points to lack of clear guidelines from policy makers on the functions or purposes of statutory reviews.

The nature of decisions: All the decisions recorded at reviews (894) were described by the researcher along seven dimensions. In brief these were: the level of impact of the decision, whether it was new, modified or a repeat, the specificity of goals and of action, the expected time scale for implementation, the focus of the content and the appropriate social work activity. One, among many, of the conclusions from this analysis suggests that against what is regarded as good decision-making practice a high proportion of these decisions were recorded in a vague way, thereby making effective monitoring of such decisions difficult.

The levels of decision implementation: In less than 10% of decisions did the social worker fail to work in some measure towards implementation; furthermore 62% of the decisions were successfully implemented — although this figure drops to 50% of decisions taken in residential homes. Two general causes emerge as the most important reasons for failure to implement; lack of co-operation of the child, the family, and other agencies, and lack of resources. This latter was particularly important for decisions taken on children in residential care which had the lowest level of successful implementation.

The place of reviews in child care practice: There is considerable confusion among social workers as to the purpose and the importance of reviews, particularly in relation to planning for children in care. Social workers are aware of the need to improve long-term planning for children in care, but are uncertain how this relates to the present review process.

Although this research focuses on an authority that has a good record in conducting reviews within the statutory requirements, on a wide range of child care cases, the researcher questions whether these reviews are being used as effectively as possible, and concludes that any further regulation of the conduct of reviews must be linked to a clear understanding of their purpose.

Social Workers and Solicitors in Child Care Cases
Linden Hilgendorf.
HMSO — 1981.

This study conducted between 1978 and 1980 was concerned with the decision to take a child into the care of a local authority under a court order. Such a decision emerges from a process which takes place over time and involves many individuals and agencies, most notably social services departments and local juvenile courts. Despite the existence of national laws and administration controls, there is considerable variation in the operation of local systems making these decisions and the ways in which individual professionals undertake their responsibilities. Social workers are key actors in the process and it is on their roles and relationships that this study was focussed.

The study took place in five local authorities. Interviews were conducted with a sample of 150 social workers and a sample of 50 private solicitors. Data on 72 cases were collected from various sources including records, interviews and observation of court hearings. The published report describes the functioning of the system over the normal range of cases that are handled by social services departments and which come before the courts, particularly drawing attention to the considerable variability in practice that exists from one authority to another. What follows is a short summary of some of the wide range of findings and suggestions for improving practices made in the report.

Social workers usually play a major part in both initiating action, preparing the case, and presenting it to the court. The role demands placed on social workers are complex and sometimes conflicting. Although many expressed anxiety and uncertainty about these cases, social workers were relatively unaware of the true complexity of their position. Some training and help was available to them but the development of support systems is not adequate.

The solicitor who handles child care cases in the legal department of the local authority plays an important part in the decision making process. Although this function has become increasingly important, sufficient attention has not been given to the nature of the role or the relationship with the social services department, problems often being created by geographical distance and the short time such solicitors stay in post.

Private solicitors are involved in many child care cases, usually representing the child. Many difficulties arise for solicitors both of a practical kind, such as inadequate time and lack of expert help for preparing the case, and as to the nature of the role he should take in proceedings which are concerned with the best interests of the child. Uncertainties and disagreements over these matters can sometimes lead to suspicion and unco-operativeness in their relationships with social workers.

Specific suggestions made in the report included: improvements to the physical setting of juvenile courts; separate scheduling of care and criminal cases; the need for all aspects of court procedure to be strictly adhered to; parents to be helped to take part in proceedings; the proper role of the solicitor representing the child to be clarified; more training for social workers in court work and child care cases; development of social services practice in dealing with solicitors; the juvenile court to have a wider range of disposal options. Overall a number of measures will be required:

(a) to shift the operational bias away from "winning a case" to planning for the future placement and care of the child, in view of the alternatives which are realistically available;

(b) to allow decisions to be made which minimise disruption and delay in the placement of the child;

(c) to ensure that the rights of the parents are respected and their access to a full and fair hearing by an independent court is guaranteed.

The Administrative Parent
A study of the assumption of parental rights and duties.
Margaret Adcock, Richard White and
Olwen Rowlands.
BAAF — 1983.

This project examined how Section 2 of the Children Act 1948 (now Section 3, Child Care Act 1980) was operating and sought to clarify the social work, legal and judicial factors which affected this. A consecutive sample of 267 cases in which Section 3 resolutions were passed was drawn from two urban and two county authorities. In addition, each local authority in England and Wales was asked how they exercised their powers to assume parental rights and what grounds had been used between 1978–81.

The main findings were:

1. The assumption of parental rights is a point at which the rights of parents and the welfare of children may conflict.

2. The researchers concluded that every child in the sample did need either protection from their parents or someone to act as an effective parent.

3. The research did not show any pattern of misuse of powers by local authorities, although given the current interpretation of Section 3(1) — the "consistent failure" ground — which requires culpability and not mere inadequacy, there is some doubt as to whether 31% of the cases involving this ground were, on a strictly legal construction of the statute, within the statutory grounds. With this exception there were only three cases in which there was doubt as to whether the grounds were made out and four where there was abuse of the procedures. There was no evidence that the consent procedure was misused, but it was clearly open to misuse. Social workers usually witnessed parents' signatures.

4. "Consistent failure" was the most frequently used ground, involving 43% of cases, in the study authorities. Nationally "consistent failure" and "three years" were almost equally used.

5. There was no evidence that the "three years" ground had served any good or necessary purpose for children, social workers or parents. In only 4 cases out of 71 where the "three years" ground was used in the study would there appear to have been any difficulties in making out a case on other grounds. (Subject to the judicial interpretation of "consistent failure".)

6. The wording of the "same household" ground, Section 3(1)c, makes it difficult for the section to be used.

7. None of the four study authorities had a written policy statement on Section 3 resolutions. In 41% of cases, a resolution was intended to stabilise the child in permanent care until 18 and in 21% of cases in indefinite care but with no stated plan. In only 27% of cases had plans been made to work towards the children leaving care through rehabilitation or adoption.

8. Communication with and information to parents on their rights in most cases was adequate (eg suggesting legal advice and explaining what powers the local authority would acquire), except over access.

9. Less than 10% of cases were actually challenged in court. When hearings were held, the hearsay rule and admissibility of evidence caused constant difficulties. Of 21 social work witnesses only 2, in the opinion of the researchers, were consistently competent. The interests of the children were often lost sight of.

10. Each of the cases was rated on ten factors to give some indication of the local authorities' ability to act as a good parent, providing consistent and reliable parenting. In only 4% of cases were there no elements of "failure" and in nearly 50% of cases there were 4 failures or more.

The Implementation of Section 56 of the Children Act 1975
(Unpublished research report)
Olive Stevenson and John Smith.

This section requires parents or guardians to give not less than 28 days notice of their intention to remove their child from care, where the child has been received into care under Section 2 of the Child Care Act 1980.

The study was designed to investigate the implementation of the section and its effects on policy and practice. Part I of the study is a retrospective analysis using questionnaires of a sample of 339 cases drawn from 11 local authorities in England. Part II used tape recorded interviews to follow up certain cases. There were 4 main elements for study: first the criteria upon which decisions were made to require or not to require notice; secondly, the processes involved; thirdly, the decision and action taken in response to receipt of notification of parents intention to remove the child from care; fourthly, the views of those involved in the working of the provision. This information was set against a background of data obtained about the families and children concerned, some of which has value in its own right.

A summary of findings cannot be comprehensive in detail in the space available. The following appear most significant for policy and practice.

1. 30% of parents had not been informed about Section 56 although this percentage was slightly lower in relation to children received into care after the implementation of the section. This was the only major point of concern about practice arising from the findings.

2. In 50% of relevant cases, a decision was taken to require notice. There were, however, marked variations between the eleven local authorities in those percentages, suggesting considerable differences in policy and practice. In general, *younger* children, especially those who had been in care before or had been in care for 2 – 3 years, were the most likely to be subject to notice. Other factors significant in the decision appeared to be based on professional assessment of the total situation, including parental responses and behaviour. Overall, it emerged that serious consideration was given to the issue, usually by more than one worker.

3. Parental attitudes to the requirement (as reported by the workers) is somewhat ambiguous. 35% were reported as 'accepting' but more detailed comment by workers suggested that apprehension, concern and hostility may lie behind bare statistics. This is an area which merits further exploration.

4. In three-fifths of cases to which Section 56 was relevant, it was enforced at the point of discharge from care. Again, the younger the child, the more likely, especially if the young child was in foster care.

5. Only 7 children (4% of the 'Section 56 applicable' sample) were 'illegally' removed by parents. Closer examination of these cases suggested that even in these few the 'illegality' was debatable, either in principle or practice.

6. Of the 296 social workers who participated, 70% had been employed for 5 years or more and 80% had a recognised qualification. In general, they did not have strong views about this provision but its use was thought about carefully

and implemented sensibly. There is, however, room for improvement in practice so that *all* parents are informed of the requirement in principle. There is also some ground for concern about policy variation between authorities which may be related to different interpretations of the 'permanency planning' strategy.

7. An incidental finding, of critical importance for child care practice, is the very large numbers of children in care who returned to differently constituted families: at least 35% and possibly as many as 50% of our total sample. This reflects to an extent demographic trends but adds a new dimension to the concept and process of rehabilitation.

Title and Authors	Description	Sample	Method
Who Needs Care? *Social work decisions about children.* Jean Packman, John Randall and Nicola Jacques. Blackwell — due Spring 1986.	Intensive study of admissions in 2 contrasting authorities. Includes those 'seriously considered' but not admitted and compares outcomes.	361 cases; all ages, all legislative routes.	Interviews with social workers and parents. Follow up at 6 months.
Children Lost in Care. *The family contact of children in care.* Spencer Millham, Roger Bullock, Ken Hosie and Martin Haak. Gower — due Autumn 1985.	A cohort study, focus on child care careers and barriers to child–parent links. Comparison between those who left quickly and those who stayed long.	450 children; all ages; all legislative routes; followed for 2 years. Intensive study of 30 cases. 5 authorities.	Records, interviews with social workers and some parents.
In Care: A study of Social Work Decision Making Jeni Vernon and David Fruin. NCB — due Autumn 1985.	Focus on whether and how decisions were made at key points of children's in-care careers.	185 children; all ages; one group coming into care and another already in care. (Excluded POSOs) Followed for 1 year. 11 authorities.	Records, interviews with social workers, attending reviews and meetings.
In and Out of Care *The experience of children, parents and social workers* Mike Fisher, Peter Marsh and David Phillips with Eric Sainsbury. Batsford/BAAF — due 1986	A study of the retrospective perceptions and experiences of care from children, parents and social workers.	79 children over 8 years old, parents and a variety of care providers. One authority.	Interviews.
Long Term Foster Care Jane Rowe, Hilary Cain, Marion Hundleby and Anne Keane. Batsford/BAAF — 1984.	A study of children growing up in foster families and the potential effect of the Children Act 1975. Comparison with those whose foster parents adopt them.	200 cases in main sample; all in this foster home a minimum of 3 years. 5 authorities.	Records, interviews with social workers, foster parents, children and natural parents.
Decision Making in Statutory Reviews on Children in Care Ruth Sinclair. Gower — 1984.	Study of process, style, functions, decisions and implementation of reviews.	Cases from one authority. Excluded v. short-term cases.	Records, questionnaires to social workers and discussions with them, observations of reviews.
Social Workers and Solicitors In Child Care Cases Linden Hilgendorf. HMSO — 1981.	A study of the process of decision making in care order cases up to and including the court hearing. Focus on roles and relationships of social workers and lawyers.	150 social workers and 50 solicitors in 5 authorities. Followed 72 cases.	Interviews.
The Administrative Parent *A study of the assumption of parental rights and duties.* Margaret Adcock, Richard White and Olwen Rowlands. BAAF — 1983.	An investigation of the use made of S.3 of the Children Act 1975.	267 children, all ages; S.3 cases only. 4 authorities.	Records, interviews with social workers, attendance at court hearings.
The Implementation of Section 56 of the Children Act 1975 (Unpublished research report) Olive Stevenson and John Smith.	A study of the use and effectiveness of the section enabling care authorities to require 28 days notice of the removal of children who have been in voluntary care for at least 6 months.	339 cases from 11 authorities.	Part 1. Retrospective study by postal questionnaire to social workers. Discussions with senior management. Part 2. Interviews with 46 social workers and a few foster and natural parents in 4 authorities.

PART III   True for Us?

The exercises and questions set out in this section are designed to provide social work managers and practitioners with a simple and varied way of considering their own, local experience and practice in the light of the research findings. There is no suggestion that their use is required or even that this would always be appropriate. The aim is to offer an opportunity to pursue the "I wonder if that applies to us?" questions that inevitably arise as one reads these reports. Looking at local practice in this way serves the dual purpose of testing the research findings and evaluating one's own performance. The results may be reassuring or may produce evidence which stimulates local change and development.

The exercises are not intended to be mini research projects or to produce statistically valid figures. Nor are they meant for routine use. Their primary value is to stimulate ideas, discussion and further enquiry. However, some of the charts might provide a helpful method of regularly recording changes. Others could be adapted for use in gathering data in a more formal and structured way either in one area or across a whole department.

It is not necessary to attempt all the exercises or to do them in any particular order. Each is planned to be used on its own and not all will be of equal relevance or interest to everyone. There is no hierarchy of importance and some of the most crucial issues raised by the research are not covered because they do not lend themselves to this sort of treatment.

Most of the exercises are best suited for use by a social work team or on training courses or study days. Some exercises could be done on a larger scale while others are mainly for the use of individuals as an aid to think about what is going on within their cases or in their team. They are not likely to work well if imposed on reluctant groups or if they are perceived as a tool for management to check up on practice.

The person presenting the exercises or leading discussion of them will need to be familiar with the findings reported in the overview and should be prepared to encounter some scepticism about research. It may be helpful to point out the wide range of authorities studied in the research projects and the near unanimity of the findings.

Copies of the charts will be found in the pocket in the back of this booklet. Some could be easily adapted for the study of other topics including those listed as additional questions. Issues of particular local concern or interest can also be added.

Although some charts are designed to accommodate 10 or 20 cases, a basis for discussion may be obtained with fewer cases. Additional charts can be used to include larger numbers. Obviously, the more rigorously and widely the exercises are done, the more valid will be the answers they provide, but interesting facts and ideas will emerge from quite limited use.

The Exercises

A) Children's social networks and family links — breaks and changes following admission to care

B) Changes in family composition

C) Preventive services

D) Departmental policies

E) Use of Place of Safety Orders

F) Who knows what about the child's history and background?

G) Admission to care — practice issues

H) Moves and separations in care

I) Reasons for admission — shared perceptions or crossed wires?

J) Stress, pain and support

(A)
Children's Social Networks & Family Links — Breaks & Changes Following Admission to Care

The Research Finding to be Tested

The importance of family links to children's well-being and to their chances of returning home again are a major theme of the Dartington research which shows the alarming rapidity with which links wither. (See Overview pages 10, 11 and 13)

The Exercise is to complete individual charts which plot the social and family networks of children and young people in care. Doing each one can be thought provoking and instructive. Study of a series may reveal patterns arising from policy and practice.

The chart could helpfully be completed by social worker (or caregiver) and child together. Alternatively, social worker, caregiver and child might each complete a chart and then compare notes.

This exercise is well adapted for use by an individual social worker, by a small team or with groups in training.It is not suitable for gathering any kind of statistical data on access or family links.

It is probably best to select cases where the child has been in care for at least a month.

A completed chart is provided as an example.

Some questions which could usefully be considered as part of the exercise include:

1) Does departmental policy encourage local placement of children so as to avoid changes of school etc?

2) What would need to be done to introduce and implement such a policy?

3) What more could be done to preserve and maintain children's links

   a) with their home neighbourhood

   b) with their former friends

   c) with their wider family network?

4) Do field and residential social workers know about children's networks and attachments? If not, does it matter?

Example: Networks and Family Links

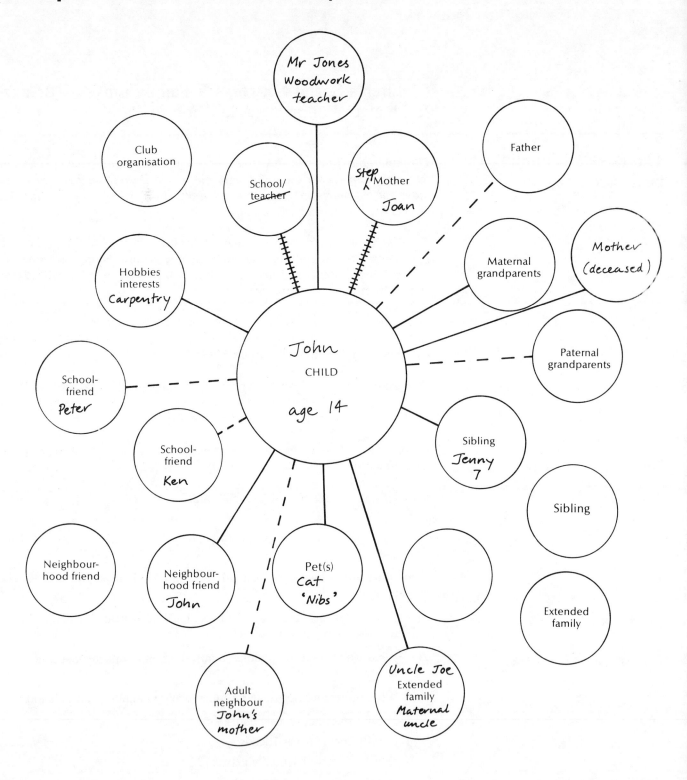

Draw in connections where they exist.

Identify important people or organisations and use blank circles as needed.

Use different type of lines to indicate the nature of the link or relationship:

——— = strong
----- = weak
////// = stressful

Chart A   Networks and Family Links

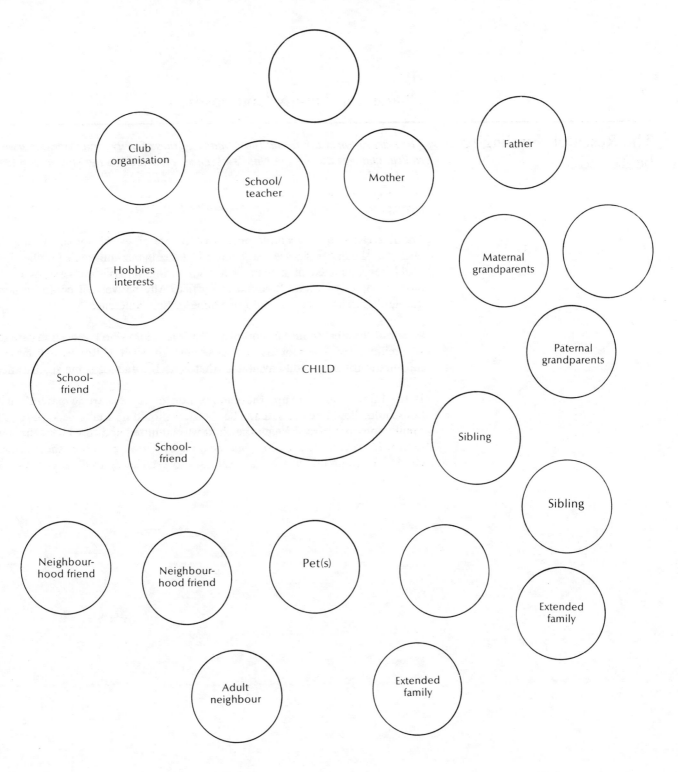

Draw in connections where they exist.

Identify important people or organisations and use blank circles as needed.

Use different type of lines to indicate the nature of the link or relationship:
—— = strong
----- = weak
++++ = stressful

(B)
Changes in Family Composition

The Research Finding to be Tested

The Dartington study found that "many of these family structures underwent radical changes during the child's absence, even though the stay in care was short...By six months, nearly half of the children will have had a major change in their family structure." Other researchers also commented on rapid changes in the households the children had left. (See Overview page 11)

The Exercise is a very simple one. It offers a framework for answering the question "I wonder if there are so many changes in *our* children's families?" It could be conducted at a team meeting, during supervision sessions or by passing copies of Chart B round the office. Alternatively, it could be done during discussion with the child or young person concerned.

A pair of 'houses' should be completed for each child who has been in care for a minimum of six months (or a sample of such children). If current information is not readily available, that is itself a fact of some significance.

If the family has split up, the composition of the departing parent's new household should be indicated. The 'houses' should normally be kept for the family household from which the child was admitted and to which s/he will return. However, the exercise could be done by allowing a whole sheet to each child and adding information as necessary to keep an up to date record of all family changes.

Chart B Changes in Family Composition

Instruction *Write the members of the child's family household in each house*

Example

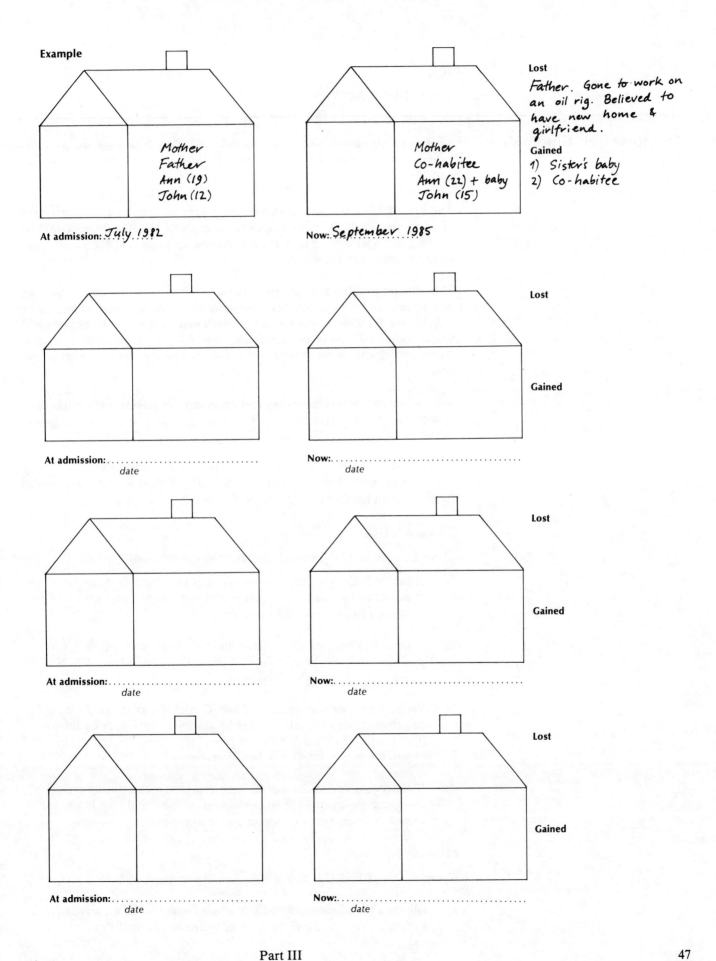

Mother
Father
Ann (19)
John (12)

At admission: *July 1982*

Mother
Co-habitee
Ann (22) + baby
John (15)

Now: *September 1985*

Lost

Father. Gone to work on an oil rig. Believed to have new home & girlfriend.

Gained
1) Sister's baby
2) Co-habitee

At admission: ....
date

Now: ....
date

Lost

Gained

At admission: ....
date

Now: ....
date

Lost

Gained

At admission: ....
date

Now: ....
date

Lost

Gained

Part III

(C)
Preventive Services

The Research Finding to be Tested

Packman reports that parents whose children had not been admitted to care often felt that nothing helpful had been offered instead. (See Overview pages 9 and 16)

The Aim of The Exercise is to demonstrate what services are provided as part of preventive work. It does not attempt to evaluate the effectiveness of these services, but does give an opportunity to show up unmet needs and, perhaps, some untapped resources.

This exercise is only likely to prove useful if participants feel free to be open and honest about their practice. Working on it should help people to be imaginative about what services clients need and what might be provided: a) when additional resources are made available; b) even within existing constraints. Participants should not feel limited to the services listed on the chart.

The 'not considered' column may carry a significant message, but it has to be appreciated that a service might be 'not considered' just because it is known to be 'not available'.

As with several of these exercises, the discussion that it is likely to stimulate may well be more important and useful than any figures that are obtained from the completed charts.

Alternative Uses

There are several ways in which this exercise can be used:

1)   It can be limited to cases where RIC was prevented *or* it can be stretched to include those where preventive services were provided but admission to care was still necessary.

2)   If your area handles a very large number of referrals for care, you may wish to limit the exercise to a particular type of case, e.g. NAI; non school attendance; delinquency.

3)   The range of services listed on Chart C could be expanded or it could be substantially reduced — either by grouping services or by limiting the list to a small number of key provisions. These might then be monitored over a larger number of cases.

4)   If supervisor and social worker each complete a chart using the same cases, a comparison of their perceptions of need and how it was (or should be) met, could be useful and illuminating.

Method

Completion of Chart C is best undertaken in two stages.

1)   Obtain a list of cases where there was a request — by a parent or someone else — for a child to be admitted to care and there was at

least one interview with the parent(s). (If the administrative/statistical system in your office is not geared to producing information on referrals, it may be necessary to use the team meeting or individual supervision sessions, to compile a list of appropriate cases.)

2) For each service listed on Chart C, the number allocated to the case should be written in a box in the appropriate section. Thus, for the first family on the list, the number 1 might be written:— in the 'provided' column for counselling; in the 'not needed' column for direct work with child; the 'not considered' column for family therapy; 'needed but not available' for holiday for parent. And so on down the list.

Chart C   Preventive Services

Instructions *Fill in family number in appropriate column for each service*

	PROVIDED				NEEDED BUT NOT AVAILABLE			NOT NEEDED/ NOT APPROPRIATE			NOT CONSIDERED		
Counselling for parent	1	2	3	5					4				
	6	7	9	10				8					
Direct work with child		2		5	1				3	4			
			9			10	6	7				8	
Family therapy		2				4			3		1		5
			9				6			10	7	8	
Behaviour modification plan				5	2				3	4	1		
			10				6	7	8				9
Group work with parents					1	2			3	4			5
		7				8	6			10		9	
Group work/IT for child		2			1			5	3	4			
			9	10			6	7	8				
Referral to other counselling agency									1	2	3	4	5
	6												
Help in obtaining medical advice/care			3										

Play group/moth—

The purpose of using a number for each family instead of just ticking the list is to make it possible to count up what was provided (or needed) for a particular family as well as getting an overall total. However, if the exercise is being used to spark discussion on a particular occasion (e.g. on a training course) and the chart will not be referred to again, it may not be necessary to allocate numbers and the boxes could just be ticked as appropriate.

Chart C is set up to accommodate 10 cases. Additional charts can be completed to build up a more accurate picture or to point up the need for a particular service. But even one chart will provide some ideas about what services are being provided and may indicate some serious gaps.

It may be useful to put the main reason for the initial referral alongside the cases on the list. This will make it possible to link the original problem with the kinds of help subsequently needed. It will also be helpful to indicate whether or not admission to care proved necessary.

Questions for discussion

Many questions will inevitably arise in the course of completing the chart. Among additional topics that might be usefully pursued are:

1) Ways of mobilising wider family support, e.g. holding family councils in the home of the person considered to be 'head of the family' by the other family members.

2) Use of volunteer visitors and local projects such as Home Start.

3) The dilemma that exploration of needs may raise hopes or expectations which cannot be fulfilled.

4) When clients request help with one problem, how far should other needs be explored?

Chart C   Preventive Services

Instructions   *Fill in family number in appropriate column for each service*

	PROVIDED	NEEDED BUT NOT AVAILABLE	NOT NEEDED/ NOT APPROPRIATE	NOT CONSIDERED
Counselling for parent				
Direct work with child				
Family therapy				
Behaviour modification plan				
Group work with parents				
Group work/IT for child				
Referral to other counselling agency				
Help in obtaining medical advice/care				
Play group/mother & toddler group etc				
Day care/child minder				
Family centre				
Holiday for parent				
Holiday for child				
Relief care				
Mobilising the extended family				
Family aide				
Volunteer visitor/organised help from neighbour				
Welfare rights/social security/ negotiations/advice				
Direct financial/material help				
Negotiation/advice re fuel debts				
Negotiation/advice re housing				
Other				
TOTAL:				

(D)
Departmental Policies

The Research Finding to be Tested

"Official policy statements were generally fragmented, partial and sometimes elusive and of uncertain status." (Packman) (See Overview pages 15 and 20)

The Exercise can be used to explore whether policies exist, are known, are accepted and used.

It can be done in a variety of groups either within a department or on a training course and it is particularly helpful if people from various levels are present.

Each member of the group will need a set of questions to complete. When this has been done, the answers should be shared and discussed. An interesting variation (and a useful one if those participating feel any awkwardness about not knowing or not fulfilling policies), is to mix up the papers and let participants read out each others'.

If time is short, it may be necessary to select just two or three questions or divide the questions up among the group.

The questions concern departmental policy on:

> Voluntary or compulsory admissions
> What S.1 money can be used for (S12 in Scotland)
> Having natural parents at reviews
> Placing children in foster families of the same
> ethnic origin
> Using RIC as part of a preventive service
> The level in the hierarchy at which decisions on RIC
> must/should be taken

Some additional or alternative questions might be about:

> Admission to care for non-school attendance
> Keeping siblings together
> Placing children within their local home area
> Use of CHEs (not applicable in Scotland)
> Use of residential establishments run by
> voluntary organisations or other authorities
> Taking S.3 Resolutions (S.16 in Scotland)

Exercise D   Departmental Policies

1)   **VOLUNTARY OR COMPULSORY ADMISSIONS**

Is there a departmental policy on this?   YES/NO   If 'YES' complete a – e
                If 'NO' complete e only

a)   What is it?_____

b)   Where is it stated? (If in a policy paper or other document, where is this kept?)

c)   Is it mandatory or just general guidance?_____

d)   Do you agree with it?_____

e)   What is your own 'policy'/practice on this?_____

2)   **WHAT S.1 MONEY CAN BE USED FOR (S.12 in Scotland)**

Is there a departmental policy on this?   YES/NO

a)   What is it?_____

b)   Where is it stated? (If in a policy paper or other document, where is this kept?)

c)   Is it mandatory or just general guidance?_____

d)   Do you agree with it?_____

e)   What is your own 'policy'/practice on this?_____

3)   **HAVING NATURAL PARENTS AT REVIEWS**

Is there a departmental policy on this?   YES/NO

a)   What is it?_____

b)   Where is it stated? (If in a policy paper or other document, where is this kept?)

c)   Is it mandatory or just general guidance?_____

d)   Do you agree with it?_____

e)   What is your own 'policy'/practice on this?_____

4) **PLACING CHILDREN IN FOSTER FAMILIES OF THE SAME ETHNIC ORIGIN**

Is there a departmental policy on this?   YES/NO

a)   What is it?_____

_____

b)   Where is it stated? (If in a policy paper or other document, where is this kept?)

_____

c)   Is it mandatory or just general guidance?_____

d)   Do you agree with it?_____

e)   What is your own 'policy'/practice on this?_____

_____

5) **USING ADMISSION TO CARE AS PART OF A PREVENTIVE SERVICE**

Is there a departmental policy on this?   YES/NO

a)   What is it?_____

_____

b)   Where is it stated? (If in a policy paper or other document, where is this kept?)

_____

c)   Is it mandatory or just general guidance?_____

d)   Do you agree with it?_____

e)   What is your own 'policy'/practice on this?_____

_____

6) **THE LEVEL AT WHICH DECISIONS ON ADMISSION MUST/SHOULD BE TAKEN**

Is there a departmental policy on this?   YES/NO

a)   What is it?_____

_____

b)   Where is it stated? (If in a policy paper or other document, where is this kept?)

_____

c)   Is it mandatory or just general guidance?_____

d)   Do you agree with it?_____

e)   What is your own 'policy'/practice on this?_____

_____

(E)
Use of Place of Safety Orders

The Research Finding to be Tested

Several of the research studies highlighted the increasing use of compulsory powers especially POSO's. For example, 20% of the Packman cohort and 30% of the Dartington cohort entered care on such orders. Some, but not all researchers found that compulsion had a negative effect on relationships between parents and social workers. (See Overview pages 7, 8 and 19)

The Exercise will be of interest to both managers and social workers in departments which use place of safety orders quite often but lack information about them. (Not suitable for use in Scotland.) It is designed to produce data on the circumstances in which these orders are used and their effect on relationships between parents and social workers. This data can then be compared with the research findings.

There are two basic, fact finding questions and a chart. You can do the questions or the chart or both. Obtaining answers to the questions will probably involve administrative staff in looking up statistical returns. Or the information might be obtained from your department's court section.

Fact Finding Question 1

During the past year, what proportion of admissions in your department/team/caseload were POSO's?

$$\text{e.g. } \frac{24 \text{ POSO's}}{120 \text{ admissions}} \times 100 = 20\%$$

Fact Finding Question 2

How many of these POSO's subsequently became care orders?

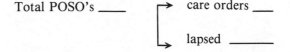

The questions which form the headings on the chart are:

1. Child's age?
2. Reason for order?
3. Who took out the order, social worker, duty officer or police?
4. If police, were S.S.D. consulted?
5. Looking back, was a Place of Safety Order essential?
6. How long did the child stay in care?

Chart B provides a method of organising more detailed information about the use of POSO's and their effects. The chart should be completed for a consecutive series of POSO's if possible. But if it proves difficult to obtain a list of such cases from administrative staff, social workers could be asked to compile the list from their own case notes or even their recollection. Chart B can accommodate up to 20 cases.

7. Was the child's main placement in a foster family or a residential establishment?
8. During the child's stay in care, what was the *prevailing* relationship of natural family to social worker?

Examination of the answers to the first seven questions should provide some beginning ideas of the sort of cases where a POSO is being used. The final question may give some indication of whether the use of compulsory orders does indeed have a negative effect on relationships between parents and social workers.

Questions can, of course, be added or deleted according to your particular interests or concerns and the time available for completion.

Chart E   Place of Safety

Child's name	Age			Reason for Order				Who took?			Police consult?		Essential?			Case known previously?			Time in care (This episode)					Type of placement			Parents' relationship with social worker		
	0-4	5-9	10-15	16+	abuse/ neglect	moral danger	delin- quency	beyond control	Police	Social Worker	Duty Officer	Yes	No	Yes	No	?	No	Yes recently	Yes at least 4 weeks	Up to 7 days	1-4 weeks	5 weeks 6 mths	over 6 mths	still in care	foster home	residential	other eg hospital	positive construc- tive	passive	negative angry suspicious

Period during which these orders were taken. From................. To.................

(F)
Who Knows What About the Child's History & Background?

The Research Finding to be Tested

Rowe's research on long-term foster care showed that foster parents often had very little information and frequently did not pass on to the children even the little that they had. Marsh and Fisher found that residential social workers were also very poorly informed on the child's background and the reasons for care. (See pages 14 and 21 of the Overview.)

The Aim of this Exercise is to help you to build up a picture of the availability and distribution of important information about children in care. It differs from most of the other exercises in two ways. Firstly, it cannot be done in the course of a team meeting or training day. It will have to be carried out over a period of time either during routine visits to residential establishments or foster homes or, possibly, as a special project. Secondly, because this is such a large topic and must encompass a variety of children in a range of care situations, it seems more appropriate to put forward a number of possible lines of approach rather than suggest one method.

During this exercise, as in any work dealing with clients' personal affairs, it is important to be constantly aware of confidentiality and the general need to seek permission before sharing information. There are also important underlying issues about accuracy, subjectivity and being clear about whose opinions are being recorded.

Selecting the Focus. If the exercise is to be done in a systematic way, it will be necessary to 'target' a particular group. This is because the purpose for which history and background data is needed will vary as will the items of information which are likely to be of most importance. Three groups can easily be identified — but there are no doubt others.

1) Children and/or adolescents who have been in care for 5 years or more. Especially if their family links have withered, they need background information to help them understand themselves and develop a secure identity.

2) Adolescents recently admitted to care. With the young person's permission, care givers should be given some background information. And both child and family may find it very helpful to sit down to discuss, explain and sort out events and relationships.

3) Young children recently admitted to care and placed in foster homes. Here detailed information is clearly essential to foster parents if they are to handle the child appropriately and sensitively but again there are issues of confidentiality and permission to divulge personal information.

Choosing the Method. The method depends on the aim. If the main aim is to establish whether or not there is a problem about information and who knows what about whom, then a fairly rapid, superficial survey will probably be the best first step. You could make yourself a simple chart, list on the left the appropriate topics (those given below or others of your choosing). Make a column for each person who should have the information e.g. yourself, the child/young person, the foster parents or the key residential worker. Make enquiries — of yourself and others — and put ticks and crosses on the chart as appropriate. If you use different coloured pens, you can fit an information profile of several children on one chart.

If you want to do an exercise that helps to gather and share information, then you need a different approach. You can, of course, use traditional methods such as discussion or forms (e.g. BAAF's Form E on the child), or written reports. But you may like to try something different.

The diagram suggested for the networks and family links exercise can be easily adapted by including factual information as well as connecting lines. An alternative is the family tree or geneogram. These are simple to do but do not expect to gather the information and get the lay-out right in one operation. Once you have the data on a rough 'tree', then you can arrange it legibly on the page. Two examples of geneograms are provided here. (The convention is to use squares for males, circles for females.)

The first, Margaret Smith's family tree, was made by a social worker, child and long-term foster parents from their combined knowledge and recollections. It is not very detailed because the available information was quite meagre. Making a geneogram shows up gaps in records especially positives and health histories. This may indicate the need for further enquiries and life story work.

The second geneogram sets out the family situation of a 14 year old boy (Darren) recently admitted to an assessment unit. It was made by the boy and his key worker over several sessions and subsequently discussed with him and his mother and her co-habitee. The example is shown in two stages (Examples 2 & 3). This sort of geneogram looks quite complicated on the printed page, but using a large sheet of paper and coloured pens transforms and clarifies.

Answers to questions such as those given below may be written on the geneogram or may emerge from studying it. E.g. connections between Darren's delinquent behaviour and the changes in his family structure and important links are evident. So are his isolation in his family household and the important role of his paternal grandmother. Questions about behaviour, discipline and attitudes will arise for discussion.

Some basic questions

For Group 1

1) Where was the child born?

2) Where and with whom did s/he live before this present placement?

3) What are the natural parents' first names and what do they look like?

4) What positive qualities, skills, interests etc do (or did) the natural parents display?

5) What are the life circumstances of the child's wider family e.g. grandparents, aunts and uncles?

6) Why (in detail) was the child admitted to long-term care?

For Group 2

1) Where and with whom did s/he live before this present placement?

2) What were relationships like with each of these people?

3) What (in detail) were the difficulties leading to the present admission?

4) How long had these been going on and what remedies have been tried?

5) What school did the child attend and how did s/he get on?

   a) at lessons
   b) with teachers
   c) with peers

6) What methods of discipline are used by the natural parent(s)?

7) Outside the immediate family circle, who are/have been the important people in the child's life and what characterised these relationships?

8) (If appropriate) How has s/he reacted to any previous separations?

For Group 3 the questions will be similar to group 2 except for question 5 which should be:

Has the child attended a play group, nursery or child minder?
If so, how did s/he get on?

   a) with adults
   b) with other children

Example 1.

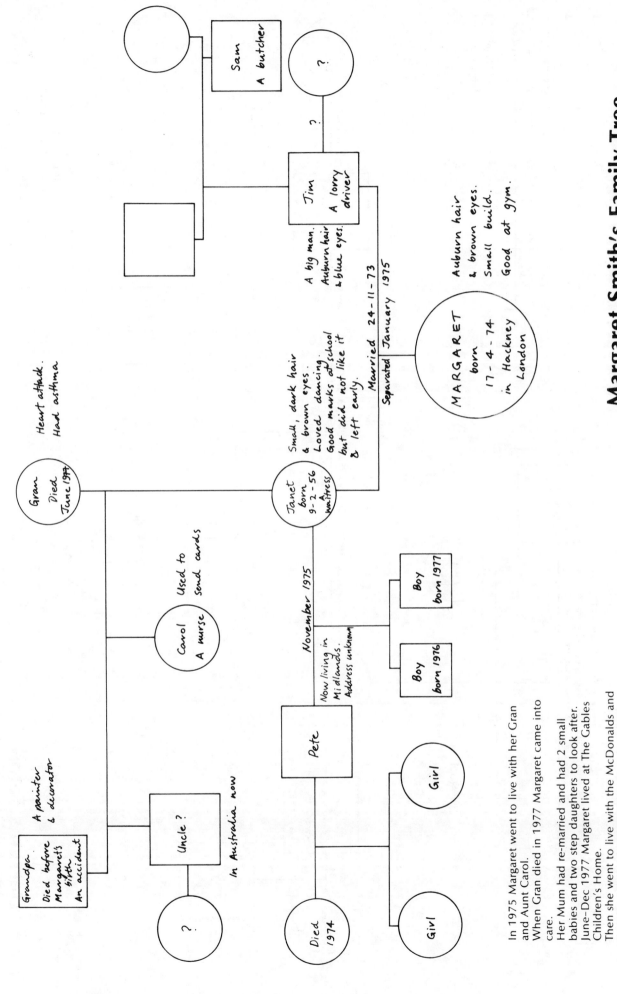

In 1975 Margaret went to live with her Gran and Aunt Carol.

When Gran died in 1977 Margaret came into care.

Her Mum had re-married and had 2 small babies and two step daughters to look after. June–Dec 1977 Margaret lived at The Gables Children's Home.

Then she went to live with the McDonalds and they have been her foster family ever since.

Margaret Smith's Family Tree

Example 2

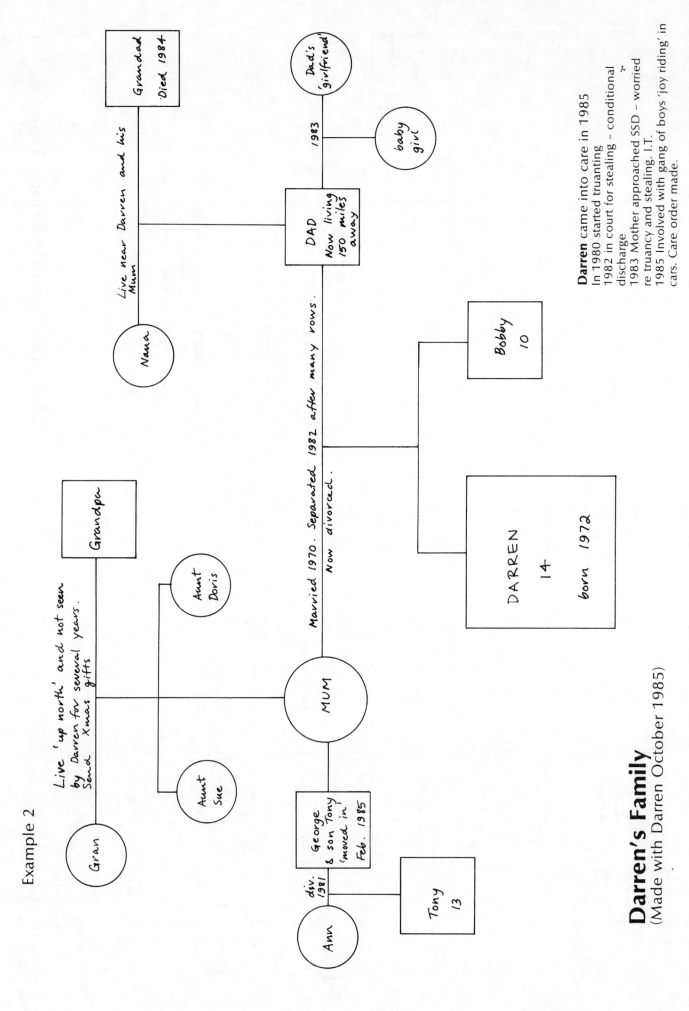

Live near Darren and his Mum

Grandad 'Died 1984

Nana

Dad's 'girlfriend'

1983

baby girl

DAD
Now living 150 miles away

Married 1970. Separated 1982 after many rows. Now divorced.

Bobby
10

DARREN
14
born 1972

Grandpa

Live 'up north' and not seen by Darren for several years. Send Xmas gifts

Aunt Doris

Aunt Sue

Gran

MUM

George & son Tony 'moved in' Feb. 1985

div. 1981

Ann

Tony
13

Darren came into care in 1985
In 1980 started truanting
1982 in court for stealing – conditional discharge
1983 Mother approached SSD – worried re truancy and stealing. I.T.
1985 Involved with gang of boys 'joy riding' in cars. Care order made.

Darren's Family
(Made with Darren October 1985)

Example 3

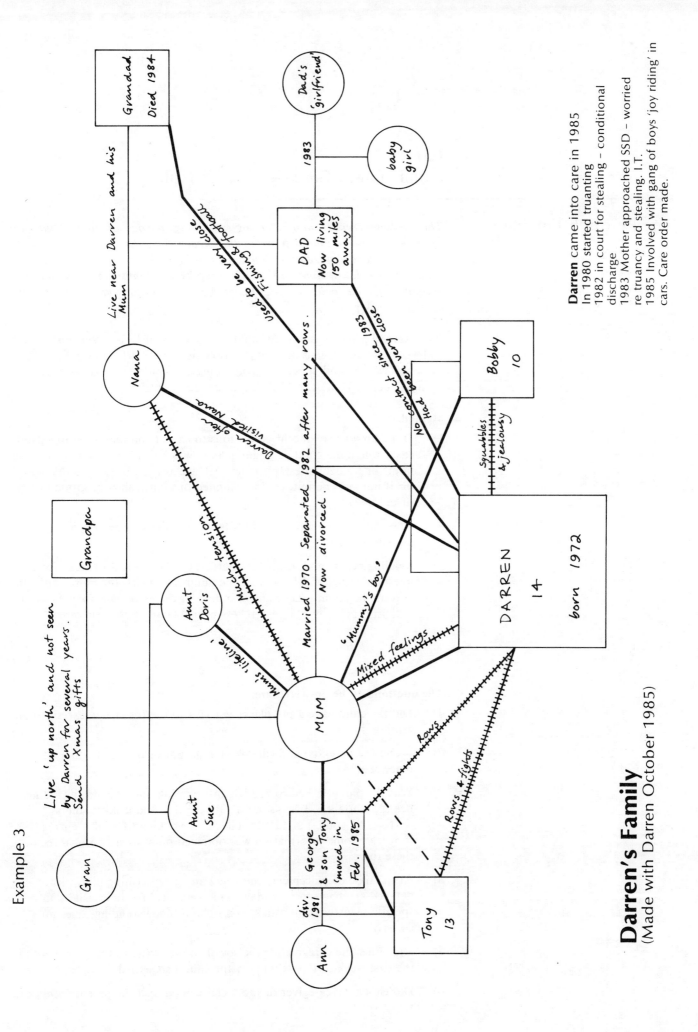

Darren's Family
(Made with Darren October 1985)

Darren came into care in 1985
In 1980 started truanting
1982 in court for stealing – conditional
discharge
1983 Mother approached SSD – worried
re truancy and stealing. I.T.
1985 Involved with gang of boys 'joy riding' in
cars. Care order made.

(G)
Admission to Care — Practice Issues

The Research Finding to be Tested

The Packman report states: "Long-established lessons of good child care practice...were honoured more in the breach than the observance." Most admissions were arranged very hurriedly and in few cases were pre-placement visits arranged. In only 15% of compulsory admissions, did parents accompany their child to the foster home or residential establishment. (See Overview page 7).

The Exercise provides a way to build up a picture of local practice strengths and weaknesses by means of a simple check list. The chart could be completed by social worker and supervisor, or during a team meeting or as part of a training course. Honesty will be important for valid findings.

Method

1) Draw up a list of recent admissions to care. (You may wish to exclude cases where the child or young person was returning to a known foster home or residential establishment.) The cases can be 'across the board' or, if numbers permit, could be limited to a particular age group or type of placement.

2) Complete one or more chart Gs by ticking the appropriate box if the answer is yes.

3) Reading across and down the chart, total the number of ticks for each question and case. The greater the number of ticks, the more confident you can be about practice in your area. If there are only a few ticks, the criticisms made by the researchers probably apply to your cases.

The questions to be answered are:

1) Did the child have a pre-placement visit to the foster home/residential establishment?

2) Did the parent(s) and caregiver(s) meet at or before the time of placement?

3) Was the parent asked to provide information on the child, including health, schooling, friends and relatives, likes and dislikes, daily routines (if young) or family rules, e.g. smoking (if adolescent)? (Tick if at least some information was obtained on at least two or three of these topics.)

4) At the time of placement, was there an agreed visiting plan with detailed arrangements for day, time, venue etc for first visit? (Only specific plans warrant a tick — a general 'understanding' does not count.)

5) Did either the caregiver or the social worker write to the parent within the first week to report on how the child had settled down?

6) Did either the caregiver or the social worker visit the parent within the first week?

Further questions

If the chart reveals a less than satisfactory picture, it may be useful to ask further questions such as:

1) For how long had the social workers for these children known about the need for placement?

2) What is really meant by 'emergency'?

3) Could the admission procedure have been slowed down or arranged differently?

4) Would it have helped if the residential social worker or foster parent had been asked to make a pre-placement visit to the child's home?

Chart G   Admission to Care – Practice Issues

Instruction   *Put a tick in the appropriate box, whenever the answer is YES.*

	Case 1	Case 2	Case 3	Case 4	Case 5	Case 6	Case 7	Case 8	Case 9	Case 10	Total ticks
Did the child have a preplacement visit?											
Did the parent(s) & caregiver(s) meet?											
Was information about routines, rules, health etc provided by parent?											
Was a visiting plan agreed?											
Did either caregiver or social worker write to the parent(s) in the first week of care?											
Did either the caregiver or social worker visit the parent(s) during the first week of care?											
Total ticks											

(H)
Moves and Separations in Care

The Research Finding to be Tested

The too frequent moves of children in care are highlighted by several of these research reports. The problem is a familiar one to social workers in a general way, but a few have a clear idea of the frequency of separations and moves for children in their own department or caseload. (See Overview page 10).

The Exercise is an adaptation of the well known flow charts often used for constructing a child's life history.

It is suggested that flow charts be constructed for a series of children who remain in care for at least six months.

The chart should indicate not only moves but all significant separations such as changes of staff or of school as well as loss of contact with family or friends. Eg. if a friend or relative stops visiting or a close friend leaves the residential establishment, this should be recorded. The exercise becomes even more revealing and useful if the main reason for any move or loss is included.

Because proper completion of these charts requires a detailed knowledge of the case, they cannot be completed from records or by administrative staff. They will be rather more difficult to do if the child's social worker has changed.

The exercise can be done by a group of social workers in a training session or team meeting. If each completes a chart for 1−3 children, it serves to heighten awareness of change and loss for children in care. Charts can usefully be prepared for reviews or case conferences.

If charts are completed for 20 or more children, it may become possible to see some patterns in the reasons for moves e.g. moves due to children's behaviour, moves due to departmental policy such as Home closures, moves from temporary placements resulting from delayed return home.

An alternative method. If you know that the child has had many moves and changes, it may be easier to arrange a flow chart in columns so that moves, changes of school and separations are linked but listed under headings (see example).

EXAMPLE

Date	Move	Change of school	Significant separations
March 1983	Sent by mother to live with father in Newtown	To John Street	From mother, sisters and friends
December 1983	Back to mother in Oldchester. (Father's co-habitee unwilling to have him any longer.)	To Chapel Hill	From father, grandmother and new friends
April 1984	(Picked up by police for vandalism) Care Order and RIC. Admitted to O & A Centre.	School in O & A Centre	From family and friends except Robert W who was RIC at same time.
May 1984	—	—	From Robert W who returned home.
July 1984	Moved to Red House Community Home.	To St. Luke's	From key worker at O & A Centre.
November 1984	—	Suspended from St. Luke's	Mother visiting less frequently. Has new boyfriend.
January 1985	—	Started at Brecknock St.	—
April 1985	—	—	From Head of Home who retired and from key worker who went off on training course.
May 1985	—	—	Grandmother died — has kept in touch regularly since RIC.

Chart H Moves and Separations in Care

Instruction *Include all changes of living place, changes of school, loss of key worker or other significant staff member, loss of friends and family through end of visits etc.*

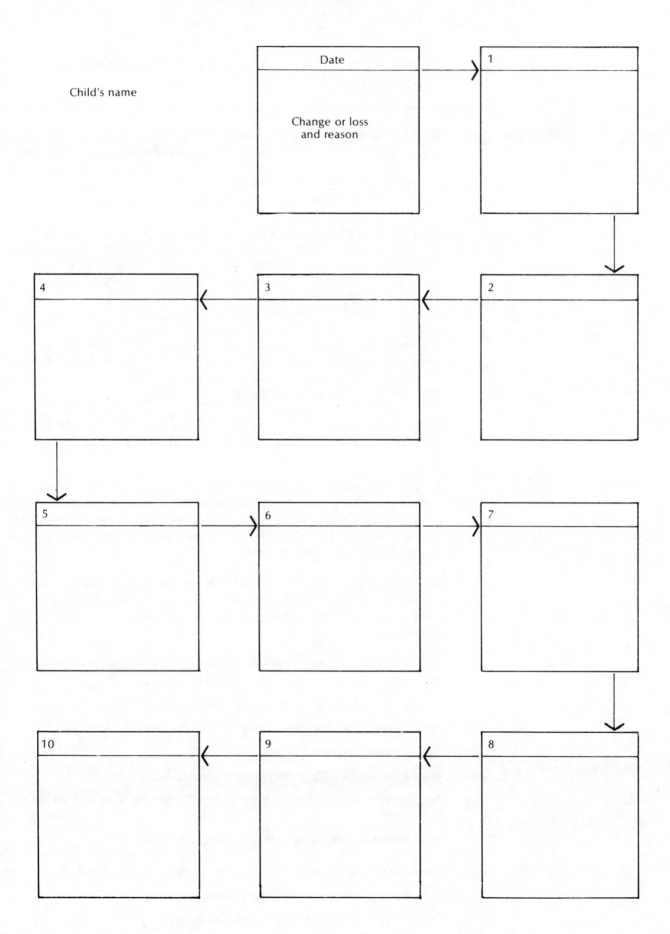

Child's name

Date

Change or loss
and reason

1

2

3

4

5

6

7

8

9

10

(I)
Reasons for Admission — Shared Perceptions or Crossed Wires

The Research Finding to be Tested

Several researchers — in particular Marsh and Fisher — point to problems caused by differing values and attitudes to child rearing held by parents, social workers and residential staff. This can lead to substantial disagreement about the <u>purpose</u> of care and to potentially serious consequences for future work and planning. (See Overview pages 8 and 17).

The Exercise is designed to explore and test out this finding in relation to the admission of teenagers. It involves the young people themselves, their parents, their field social worker and foster parent(s) or residential social worker(s) — or some combination of these people. It should be undertaken fairly soon after admission either during a special meeting, at a review, during an interview or on any occasion when several "participants" are together.

The exercise is basically very simple but requires a little advance thought and preparation each time it is used. The idea is to get the participants to list and put in order of importance the reasons for/purpose of the child's admission to care. The lists can then be compared.

Probably the best method is to give everyone 5 or 6 cards or slips of paper and ask them to write a reason on each and then arrange them in order of importance.

An alternative method (which can be used if participants are likely to have real difficulty in writing down their ideas), is to provide each participant with a set of cards with reasons already written on all but one or two of them. They should be asked to discard any that do not apply and to use the blank cards for any reasons which are not covered.

Whichever method is used, the production of very different lists is likely to indicate a potentially dangerous confusion of purpose and the need for clarification and very careful planning. It will also confirm the research finding.

The following are some "reasons" which were quite frequently expressed by parents and teenagers in the Marsh & Fisher study:

1)   To teach him/her a lesson and some respect for parents

2)   So that I can have more things and go out like my friends do

3)   To stop us quarrelling with one another

4)   To make him/her value the things he/she has at home

5)   Because we can't get on when we're all under the same roof all the time

6)   Because I want to be able to see my own friends

Some additional reasons which are often given by social workers are:

7)   To help him/her toward independence.

8)   To provide more structure and consistency.

Please note. These reasons are listed to give you a start, but they will not cover all situations so you will need to make alterations and additions as seems appropriate. Always leave in one or two reasons that probably do not apply so that people have something to discard.

(J)
Stress, Pain and Support

The Research Finding to be Tested

In the eleven departments they studied, the National Children's Bureau found little formal recognition of the stressful nature of the work or the consequent need for support. Implicitly at least, the same message came through from the other studies and it is evident that the pain and grief of clients also tends to be insufficiently recognised. (See Overview pages 15, 19, 20 and 21).

The Exercise is primarily intended for managers especially senior social workers, team leaders and area directors. It poses a series of questions which could be considered and discussed by individuals or by groups of managers either formally or informally. The aim is to raise and explore some basic issues about pain, about stress, support and morale and about the roles of social workers and management.

After questions 4, 6, 7 & 8 have been considered by senior staff, it will be instructive to seek the views of field and residential workers on these topics and then compare them with those of management.

The questions

1) What evidence do you have about whether the social workers for whom you are responsible:

 a) recognise the pain, grief and loneliness felt by parents and children in the separations of the care experience;

 b) offer parents and children help with this distress?

2) Do you think it should be part of a social worker's job to work in this way?

3) If you think that the answer to question 2 is 'yes' but that it is not being done, what steps might be taken to make such work possible?

4) How would you describe the morale of your team/area at present? (You might like to write down the evidence for your views and perhaps share this with your colleagues.)

5) How many of your staff had periods of sick leave last year? Are there other signs of stress and 'burn out' e.g. constant lateness, depression, unwillingness to consider new work or new ways of working etc?

6) Which of the following are at present offering a useful source of support:

 Team meetings
 Informal groups round the coffee machine or in the pub
 Individual friendships/groupings
 Supervision sessions
 Strong administrative back-up
 Training — internal or external
 Other sources?

7) Are panels, reviews, case conferences etc expected to have a major responsibility to offer support and share the anxiety of child care decisions? Do they succeed in this?

8) Is there a creative/supportive dialogue with central management and if so, do your social workers feel part of this?

9) The following are some rather usual but essentially negative team responses to stress. Do any apply?

> Blame the management/the government
> Emphasis on bureaucratic responses
> A 'macho' attitude to problems
> Navel-gazing introspection leading to depression
> A constant search for the latest theory or method which will 'fix it'
> Avoid seeing the problem and carry on regardless

10) Do you see evidence of:

a) mutual support and general co-operation

b) co-operative working patterns e.g. shared cases or work with groups

c) personal concern for colleagues?

11) Have you considered making systematic enquiries among the staff in your team/area about:

a) areas of their work which they find most stressful where additional support or training would help

b) aspects of the working environment that may be adding to staff pressure, frustration and stress.

12) Who helps you with your own stress? What can you do about it?

Printed in the United Kingdom for Her Majesty's Stationery Office
by Commercial Colour Press, London E7.
Dd.240290 C.50 3/87